Family Fun Times

Activities that bind marriages,   build families,

and develop Christian leaders

Written by Wayne Rickerson
Edited by Theresa Hayes
Art by Mikki Klug

STANDARD PUBLISHING
Cincinnati, Ohio   3187

Library of Congress Cataloging-in-Publication Data

Rickerson, Wayne.
  Family fun times.

1. Family—Religious life. 2. Family recreation.
I. Title.
BV4526.2.R534   1987   249   86-23124
ISBN 0-87403-207-5

Foreword

I believe strongly that the home is the training center for leadership in God's kingdom. My own motivation for leadership came from the example of my parents, and I can think of many other Christians who can trace their motivation and training for leadership to their families.

If it is true that the home is the center of leadership training for our children, then it only makes sense to sharpen our focus. This book's double purpose is to help your family learn about God's plan for leadership while building a stronger family through fun and togetherness.

The activities in this book attempt to create leadership-training situations while allowing families to have fun together and enjoy one another. You will not find deep theological statements on leadership but will enjoy profound, simple truths that can be applied to people of all ages.

The cost of leadership training in your home is commitment and time; a commitment to seeing your children become effective leaders for Christ and a willingness to set aside regular, quality family time to learn together. I believe God will bless your efforts as He produces leaders for His church.

— *Wayne Rickerson*

Table of Contents

Part 3: Leadership Qualities

Part 4: Leaders Are Grateful

Part 5: Leaders Rejoice and Follow Christ

Part 6: Leaders Cooperate With One Another

Section Three—Just for Family Fun and Togetherness

Leadership in the Home

I did not know it at the time, but when I was growing up I was enrolled in a leadership-training school. That school was my home. My parents, Don and Fay Rickerson, long-time ministers and missionaries, were teaching me how to be a leader. How did this happen? By their example. I saw them live a life of servanthood to bring people to Christ, and from them I learned what it meant to be a servant/leader.

One leadership quality I learned in our home leadership-training school was trust. I watched my parents demonstrate remarkable trust in God. They believed that through God they could do anything—including going to the mission field for the first time at the age of fifty-five.

Another leadership quality I learned from my parents was love. I experienced their love, which was motivated from their relationship with Christ. It was this love that drew me into the ministry of our Lord.

Leadership training by example was not a new concept created by my parents. God saw fit to have his Son train leaders for the church by example. Jesus demonstrated by His life what it meant to be a leader. He took twelve average men and turned them into mighty leaders. His method for leadership training was, "Follow me and I will make you fishers of men."

Section One:

THE FOUNDATION

Our Heavenly Father's Example

Let's look at eight leadership qualities that our Heavenly Father possesses. These are qualities that we should be developing in our own lives, and in the lives of our family members. These eight qualities (and related Scriptures) are listed below. Read the Scriptures and rate yourself on a scale of one to ten, with ten being the best.

	Rate Yourself		*Scripture*
low	medium	high	
1 2 3	4 5 6 7	8 9 10	I have unconditional love. (1 John 4:16; 5:11-13, Psalm 89:1, 2)
1 2 3	4 5 6 7	8 9 10	I show compassion. (Psalm 103:13)
1 2 3	4 5 6 7	8 9 10	I know my child(ren). (Psalm 139:1-3)
1 2 3	4 5 6 7	8 9 10	I accept my child(ren). (Psalm 103:14)
1 2 3	4 5 6 7	8 9 10	I have time for my child(ren). (Psalm 34;4)
1 2 3	4 5 6 7	8 9 10	I meet the basic needs of my child(ren). (Matthew 7:11)
1 2 3	4 5 6 7	8 9 10	I love righteousness. (Psalm 11:7)
1 2 3	4 5 6 7	8 9 10	I discipline my child(ren) in love. (Hebrews 12:5-13)

After you have rated yourself, use the results to set some leadership goals for yourself. Find your weakest areas and take steps to strengthen them.

What I will do to strengthen:

Area 1 _____

_____

Area 2 _____

_____

Area 3 _____

_____

Our Example

The most potent leadership-training tool we have at our disposal is our example. As Jesus trained by living with His disciples, we train by living with our children. Our children learn first by what they see. They will lead like they are led. Deuteronomy 6:4-9 clearly shows this, "Hear, O Israel! The Lord our God, the Lord is one! ⁵ And you shall love the Lord your God with all your heart and with all your soul and with all your might. ⁶ And these words, which I am commanding you today, shall be on your heart; ⁷ and you shall teach them diligently to your sons and shall talk of them when you sit in your house and when you walk by the way and when you lie down and when you rise up. ⁸ And you shall bind them as a sign on your hand and they shall be as frontals on your forehead. ⁹ And you shall write them on the doorposts of your houses and on your gates."

Notice that verses five and six say that parents are *first* to love God and have God's Word in their own hearts. This will result in teaching by example. Children will learn to be servant/leaders as they see Godly qualities in our hearts. If they do not see us living out those qualities, then no amount of training will be successful. Children believe what they see, not what we tell them.

Verses seven through nine go on to explain that once we are good models for our children, then we need to "teach them diligently" (structured or formal teaching of God's Word) and "talk of them" (informal teaching of God's Word).

But I'm Not a Leader

"But I'm not a leader," I can hear some of you saying. "How can I teach by example? Often we think of leaders as those who are dynamic, strong, natural leaders. God, however, has often used people who did not possess great natural wisdom or leadership abilities. Paul says this so well in 1 Corinthians 1:26, 27, "For consider your calling, brethren, that there were not many wise according to the flesh, not many mighty, not many noble; but God has chosen the foolish things of the world to shame the wise, and God has chosen the weak things of the world to shame the things which are strong."

God's leaders come in all shapes and sizes. Some are behind-the-scenes. Some are dynamic. But God can use all of us to lead in some way. My definition of leadership is, "One who serves in such a way as to help others see the glory of Christ." Jesus himself said, "You know that the rulers of the Gentiles lord it over them, and their great men exercise authority over them. It is not so among you, but whoever wishes to become great among you shall be your servant, and whoever wishes to be first among you shall be your slave; just as the Son of Man did not come to be served, but to serve, and to give His life a ransom for many" (Matthew 20:25-28). By this definition, we can all be leaders.

Conclusion

This book is to help you mothers and fathers increase your effectiveness in developing leadership qualities in your children. Don't be overwhelmed by the task. Remember that God is at work in your children. The activities in this book will also help you identify your own leadership qualities, as you help your children develop theirs.

How Family Fun Times Can Develop Leadership

Family Togetherness

One of the things missing in many Christian homes today is a sense of family togetherness. Families are simply not taking time to do things together. There are so many activities competing for our time —work, church, school, social meetings, etc. But the fact remains that it is *very important* for families to spend time together—talking, laughing, doing things together.

I will always be thankful that Janet and I decided early in our marriage to make family fun and togetherness a priority. We consistently planned family activities including a once-a-week family night. Family night happened on Wednesday evening and it was a rare occasion when we missed. The evening usually consisted of a Christian family activity similar to the ones in this book, something to do just for fun, and a special dessert. For thirteen years we had regular family nights with the entire family. Although our older two girls—Heidi, twenty-one and Liesl, twenty—are living in another city, we still have family nights with Bridget, our sixteen-year-old daughter.

When I see the enthusiasm that Heidi and Liesl have for coming home and their desire for some good old family fun and togetherness, all the effort seems worthwhile. Our hope is that our girls will carry on the traditions of togetherness with their own families.

Doing things together as a family sets a climate for teaching Christian values in the home. When you combine teaching and family fun you have a winner!

How to Use This Book

I would like to suggest that if you do not have a regular family night you decide now to start one. It is certainly not necessary to have *regular* family nights to be able to successfully use the activities in this book, but an evening set aside each week would be a valuable asset.

Christian Family Fun Times

You will notice that the heart of this book, section two, contains twenty-one "Christian Family Fun Times." These family times focus on various aspects of leadership. Each Christian Family Fun Time has a topic Scripture and several activities from which to choose. *You do not have to do all the activities.* In most cases I have given a wide variety of activities so you can choose the ones that best meet the needs and ages of your children.

Successful Family Fun Times

To make these family times a success, I would like to emphasize two important principles. First and foremost, make these family times *fun*. The greatest mistake parents can make is to be too serious. Children want to have fun. If you make the time as enjoyable as possible, then the children will learn. If your family times are too tense or formal, then everyone will be miserable. To have fun you must be relaxed and informal. Sit on the floor or wherever you are most comfortable. Allow for diversions. We found that we seldom stick right to the topic. When interesting subjects come up, even though they are unrelated to the topic, talk about them anyway.

The second important principle is *participation.* For family fun times to be successful, each family member needs something to do. For example, one person can lead one of the activities, another person pray, and yet another family member can serve the dessert. There are enough activities within a Christian Family Fun Time to have several family members lead activities.

Developing Leadership

I suggest allowing a different family member to lead a Christian Family Fun Time each week. This is an excellent way for your children to start to develop group leadership skills. Even children as young as five or six can with some help lead a Christian Family Fun Time.

Choose one of your children to lead the family time. Tell him/her it is his responsibility to choose the activities for the family fun time that he believes the family will enjoy. It is also his responsibility to ask other family members to do certain things for the family fun time. The rule is that each family member must have a task. To help your child organize the family time, give him a index card to write down what is going to happen and what responsibilities each person has. Following is an example:

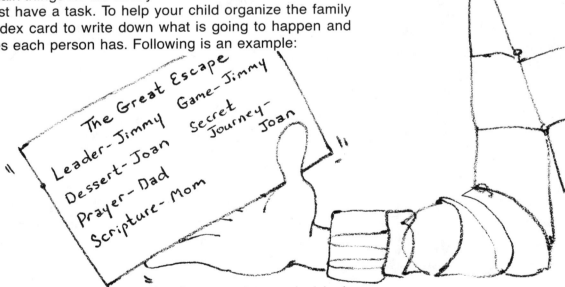

The Great Escape
Leader- Jimmy   Game- Jimmy
Dessert- Joan   Secret Journey- Joan
Prayer- Dad
Scripture- Mom

Check with your child before your family fun time to make sure he/she is organized. Sometimes the children need some guidance but let them do as much as possible by themselves.

When it comes time to have your family fun time, be sure to let the leader lead. It is a temptation to step in when we see our children struggling but they will learn by their struggles. Let a different family member lead each week.

THE GREAT ESCAPE

Leader

_____

Dessert

_____

Prayer

_____

Scripture

_____

Pharaoh's
Escape
Tag

_____

Secret
Journey

_____

The topics of the family fun times are designed to develop leadership in your children. As your family looks at the lives of great biblical leaders and examines leadership qualities, each member should improve in his/her leadership abilities.

Just for Family Fun and Togetherness

The final section of this book is to give your family some ideas for fun activities. Most of these activities are not connected to any particular biblical principle. The purpose of this section is to encourage your family to keep doing things together. Many of these activities are enjoyable enough to do over and over again.

Conclusion

I hope your family will enjoy the activities in this book so much that you will want to continue having regular Christian Family Fun Times. I would love to see regular family fun times become a tradition for your family. Have fun!

Part 1: Learning From Great Leaders

In this group of six family fun times, you will look at the lives of six great leaders from the Bible. It is in God's Word that we discover what it means to be a Godly leader. The outstanding leadership qualities of these six people can help each of your family members become better leaders.

Section Two:

FAMILY FUN TIMES

**Jesus,
the Leader
Who Was a
Servant**

**Family Fun Time
Number**

Servant Pantomime

During Jesus' three-year ministry He served in many ways. He healed the sick, He fed the hungry, He even washed His disciples feet. Have family members use their Bibles and find an place where Jesus was a servant. Then in turn, each family member is to pantomime (silently act) Jesus serving. The rest of the family is to try and guess what Jesus is doing. When a person guesses correctly, the next family member pantomimes. When the pantomimes are finished, discuss the following: Why did Jesus, the Son of God, come to earth to serve? Why did Jesus not come as a King who others would serve? Why is it important for us to serve others? Have each family member rate themselves as a servant on a scale of one to ten with ten being the highest rating.

Servant Project

Read Philippians 2:4-7. Discuss what these verses have to say about your family members becoming servants. Plan together a servant project that you can complete now or in the near future. You could bake some cookies and take to a nursing home or to an older person in your church. You could decide on something that needs to be done in the church building—cleaning, painting etc. You could take a food box to a needy family. Be creative. Think of some way your family can be servants.

World's Greatest Servant

Have each family member nominate someone they know to be the "World's Greatest Servant." Discuss as a family these nominees and their qualities. Choose one to be the "World's Greatest Servant." Make a card to send to that person. On the card have a Scripture verse about servanthood and explain why you have voted them the "World's Greatest Servant." It might look something like this:

Goal:
To help family members see that the most important quality of leadership is servanthood, and to start becoming a servant. Choose from the activities those that best suit the needs of your family.

World's Greatest Servant Award

To _Dad_

For _being patient with me when I make mistakes, and for taking the time to show me how to do it right._

Scripture _Fathers, do not exasperate your children; instead, bring them up in the training of the Lord_ _Eph. 6:4_

Signed _Jimmy_

You may make copies of this card for your family's use.

World's Greatest Servant Award

To _____

For _____

_____

_____

Scripture _____

_____

Signed _____

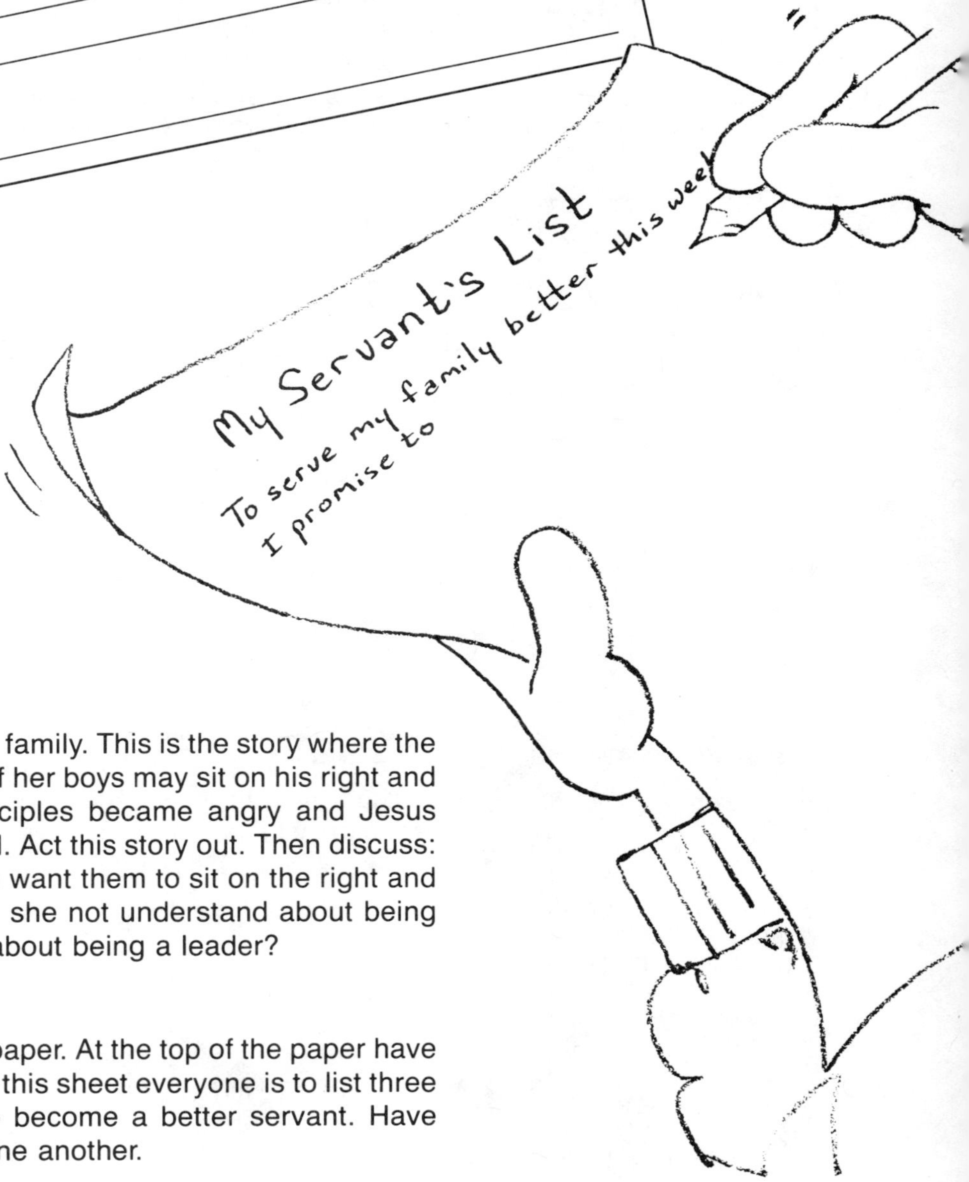

My Servant's List

To serve my family better this week
I promise to

A Servant's Play

Read Matthew 20:20-28 together as a family. This is the story where the mother of James and John asks Jesus if her boys may sit on his right and left hand in Heaven. Jesus' other disciples became angry and Jesus taught them all a lesson on servanthood. Act this story out. Then discuss: Why did the mother of James and John want them to sit on the right and left side of Jesus in Heaven? What did she not understand about being great? What does this story say to us about being a leader?

My Servant's List

Give each family member a sheet of paper. At the top of the paper have everyone write, "My Servant's List." On this sheet everyone is to list three things they will do during the week to become a better servant. Have family members share their lists with one another.

Joseph, the Leader Who Forgave

Family Fun Time Number

2

Life of Joseph Frieze

Work together as a family to create a life of Joseph frieze. (A frieze is a series of pictures that tell a continuous story.) I suggest getting a roll end from your local newspaper office. Or butcher paper. Mark off two five-foot sections. If you do not have large sheets of paper you could use five eight and one half-inch by eleven-inch sheets of paper. Plan your frieze together. The five scenes are: 1) The coat of many colors (Genesis 37); 2) Joseph in the pit and being sold (Genesis 37); 3) Joseph ruling Egypt (Genesis 42:39-45); 4) Joseph's brothers being accused of stealing (Genesis 42); 5) Joseph forgiving his brothers (Genesis 45).

If your family members are old enough, you could assign one picture of the frieze to each of them. They could each read the Scripture and draw the picture. When the frieze is completed, have each person, starting with the person who drew the first picture, could tell his or her part of the story.

When the frieze has been completed and the story told, discuss the following: Why did Joseph's brothers hate him so? How did Joseph feel when his brothers put in him the pit and then sold him? How would you have felt? How did Joseph feel in Egypt away from his family? Why do you think that Joseph forgave his brothers? Could you forgive someone if they did that to you? Why is it important for a leader to forgive others?

"Joseph and His Brothers" Play

Using the scenes from the frieze, some families might want to act out the story of Joseph. When you have completed the play, use the same discussion questions that are used with the frieze.

When Forgiving is Difficult

Forgiving is usually difficult but sometimes it is *extremely* difficult to forgive someone. Joseph's brothers were going to kill him and then they actually sold him to foreigners. But Joseph, being a great leader, was able to finally forgive his brothers. Have each family member think of the most difficult thing he or she has ever forgiven. Have each person share the story and whether he or she has really forgiven the offender. Have a circle of prayer with each person asking God to help them to forgive completely.

What the Bible Has to Say About Forgiveness

The following Bible verses talk about forgiveness. Read them aloud as a family. Next assign a verse to each family member and have him/her paraphrase that verse. By paraphrase, I mean putting the verse into his or her own words. Read these paraphrases aloud. Based on these verses, work out a family definition of forgiveness.

Scriptures: Matthew 6:12, 14, 15; Mark 11:25, 26; 2 Corinthians 2:10, 11 and Ephesians 4:32.

Goal:
To help family members understand that forgiveness is a quality of all great leaders and to help each person become more forgiving. Choose from the activities those that best suit the needs and interests of your family.

Seventy Times Seven

It is very difficult to forgive the same person time and time again, but when Peter asked Jesus how many times we must forgive, He said, "seventy times seven." That's 490 times, but what Jesus really meant was that there is no limit to the amount of times we are to forgive a person.

Here is an activity that will help family members get a sense of how difficult it is to forgive someone for the same offense time and time again. Have one family member be the "pusher" and another person the "forgiver." The "pusher" is to push the "forgiver" (gently or this can get out of hand). Each time the pusher pushes, the forgiver is to say, "I forgive you." Let this procedure go on for one minute. At the end of this time have the people reverse roles. Let each family member have a turn being a pusher and a forgiver.

Next read Matthew 18:21, 22. Talk about how difficult it was to keep forgiving over and over. Discuss how it is possible to forgive a person who keeps offending you.

Nehemiah, the Leader Who Knew How to Work

Family Fun Time Number 3

Preparing for Your Activities

It will be necessary for your family to know a little about Nehemiah and the time in which he lived before doing the "building block" activities that follow.

In 586 B.C. Babylon invaded Jerusalem and took the people captive. They destroyed the temple and tore down the wall that protected the city. The Jews who were not killed were taken to Babylon as slaves.

Some years later, Babylon was captured by the Kingdom of Persia. King Cyrus of Persia let the Jews go back to Jerusalem to rebuild the temple. The temple was rebuilt, but the wall was still in a pile of rubble.

Nehemiah, the king's cupbearer (a very important job), heard from some friends that the people in Jerusalem were in great trouble because of the broken-down wall. Nehemiah asked the king for permission to go rebuild the wall. The king said, "Yes."

Just as He did for Nehemiah, God has a task for each of us! During this family time, we will discover how to do these tasks successfully. Nehemiah's life shows us four principles on how to be a successful worker for God. We will call these principles "building blocks."

A good way to handle this family time is to have a different family member lead one of each of the following "building block" activities.

Build a Wall

Before discussing each of the following principles, make a "building block" for the wall. There are four principles so there will be four "building blocks."

Fold a regular eight-and-one-half-inch by eleven-inch piece of paper lengthwise. Write principle one on it. When you are ready to discuss principle two, follow the same procedure. Insert "building block" two into "building block" one about one inch and secure with a paper clip at the top. Repeat this procedure with the final two "building blocks" and you will have completed your wall.

Goal:
To help family members learn good work habits from a leader who knew how to work. Choose from the activities those that best suit the needs of your family.

Building Block #1
Do Each Job Well

Make "building block" one. Nehemiah was King Artaxerxes' cupbearer. A cupbearer's job was to taste the king's wine and food before the king ate or drank. This was done to make sure that someone was not trying to poison the king. Nehemiah did his job well. The king trusted him. It was doing this job well that allowed Nehemiah to do an important job for God.

Give each family member a sheet of paper. Have each of them list the tasks they are now involved in and then rate themselves on how well they do. (See the example on the right.) Beside each task write a number from one to ten. The scoring is as follows:

poor   average   good
1 2 3 4 5 6 7 8 9 10

When scoring, ask yourself the following questions: Do I finish the task? Do I do the task without grumbling? Do I try to do my best?

When family members have completed the self-evaluation, have each person share his or her results. Ask each person to select one task where his or her performance is low and think of one way to improve in that area.

My Tasks   How I Rate

Clean my room _____
Feed Scruffy _____
Wash the dishes _____
Finish my homework _____
Obey Mom and Dad _____
Water the plants _____

Building Block #2
See What Needs to Be Done

Make "building block" two and fasten it to number one. Read Nehemiah 1:1-4. Nehemiah asked some friends about his fellow countrymen in Jerusalem. When he heard that the wall was broken down he *saw* the need. Sometimes we don't "see" work because we don't want to. Perhaps we don't want to get involved.

Do the following family eye-opener: Your task is to take a sheet of paper and think of as many things as possible in five minutes that you can do for God. At the end of this activity have each person choose one thing he *will* do for God.

Building Block #3 Plan Your Work

Make "building block" three and fasten it to two. The first step in planning is prayer. Notice that Nehemiah prayed (1:4-11). Prayer and planning go together. When we pray, we make sure that God's plans are our plans.

Next Nehemiah planned his work. The king allowed Nehemiah to take a leave of absence and travel 800 miles to Jerusalem to rebuild the wall. Read Nehemiah 2:7-9. Nehemiah had a very specific plan of action.

Now is your chance to plan your work. In the previous activity you chose one thing you would do for God. Give each person a few minutes to pray about this. Then let family members plan how they're going to do their work for God. Be specific. At the end of this time share your plans with one another.

Building Block #4 Complete Your Work

Complete your wall by connecting block three to four and four to one. It is sometimes easy to start jobs but hard to complete them. Because Nehemiah felt his job was extremely important, he prayed, had a plan, and completed this huge task in fifty-two days.

Nehemiah had his share of problems. Many enemies did not want him to complete the wall. But he overcame all opposition to complete the job.

Each of us have "walls" that we need to complete for God. If we are willing to learn a lesson from Nehemiah, we will accomplish great things for God.

Take a few minutes as a family to thank God for Nehemiah and the example he has left for us.

Esther, the Leader Who Risked Her Life

Family Fun Time Number

4

Goal:
To help family members see how God uses those who are willing to take risks to carry out His will and to encourage each person to become a "risk taker." Choose the activities that best suit the needs of your family.

Diary of a Queen

This family fun time is all about Queen Esther (Esther 1-10). It is important to know the story of her life before doing the following activities. Either have someone tell the story of her life, or read the following diary.

Highlights From My Diary, by Queen Esther

—Today I heard that Queen Vashti disobeyed King Ahasuerus. The king became so angry that she is no longer queen. I heard some of the women in the market place say that there is going to be a great search for a beautiful woman to replace her.

—I just can't believe it! My Uncle Mordecai, with whom I live, entered me in a contest of girls from whom one is to become queen! I have been chosen to go to the palace where I will live for one year with some other girls learning to become a queen. Then King Ahasuerus will choose one of us.

—I really didn't think I had much of a chance of being queen but—today it happened—King Ahasuerus placed the crown on my head. It doesn't seem real. The king does not know that I am a Jew—I hope that doesn't cause problems later on.

—Last night, Uncle Mordecai told me that he heard two men talking about killing the king. I told the king and the two men will be put to death.

—I heard terrible news today. Uncle Mordecai refused to bow down to Haman, the man the king had made ruler over all the princes. Now Haman has gotten the king to agree to kill not only Mordecai but *all* Jews. There is even a chance that I will be killed!

—Last night I did not sleep at all. I must tell the king about wicked Haman. But if I go to the king and he does not hold out his scepter to me, I will be killed. That is a rule of our land. I am terribly afraid.

—I went to the king and he *did* hold out his scepter! I asked him to hold a feast and invite Haman.

—One of my servants told me that last night King Ahasuerus couldn't sleep. He had the records of the kingdom read to him. He discovered that my uncle Mordecai was not rewarded for saving his life. He has ordered wicked Haman to dress Mordecai in a royal robe and crown and parade him on a horse in the streets proclaiming, "Thus is shall be done to the man the King desires to honor."

—Today at the feast I told the King that wicked Haman was planning to kill all of my people, the Jews. The King was furious. He has ordered Haman killed on the gallows he prepared for the Jews.

—Today I'm thinking of all the things that have happened. I am amazed that God could use me, a simple Jewish girl, to save His people.

The King and I Game

Select one person to be king. Have the king sit on a throne and give him or her a scepter (rule or stick covered with aluminum foil). Each family member, in turn, may approach the king with a request in mind. If the king reaches out his scepter, the person states his request. If the king does not reach out his scepter the person must leave the room and await his death.

After the game discuss the following: How would you feel if you really took the risk of approaching a king knowing that if he did not reach out his scepter you would be killed? How do you think Queen Esther felt? Why was Queen Esther willing to take the risk? What risk have you taken because you knew something was right? Have each person share one risk they will take for God.

An Interview with Queen Esther

The whole world has heard about Queen Esther's great risk. Reporters have come from different countries to find out what would make a Queen risk her life for a small group of people.

Choose one person to be Queen Esther and the other family members will be reporters. Each reporter is to make up some questions to ask the queen. Interviewers could ask such questions as, "Why did you take the risk?" "Did you feel that God would help you?" "Do you feel that God will help other people who take risks?" "What would you say to people who are afraid to take risks?" and "How can one come to know God better?"

Risks Takers Hall of Fame

We can be thankful to God for persons who have been willing to take risks for God's sake. Make a list of "risk takers." These might be Bible characters but don't forget other Christians throughout the ages. Also think of persons who are currently living who you feel are "risk takers" for God. After you have completed your lists, have a time of prayer thanking God for all those who have taken risks for Him.

David, the Leader Who Was Not Afraid

Family Fun Time Number

5

Goal:
To help family members discover how they can overcome fear by trusting in God. Choose from the activities those that best suit the needs of your family.

Story of David and Goliath

Have someone prepared to tell or read the following story of David and Goliath.

David was a strong, good-looking young man who took care of his father's animals. David's brothers were in the Israelite army, fighting the Philistines. One day, David's father sent him with food to give to his brothers. When David arrived, the army of the Israelites were on one hill and the army of the Philistines were on another hill with a valley between them. The Philistines had a giant named Goliath whose height was nine feet, nine inches tall. He would shout at the Israelite army, "Send a man to fight me. If I win you will become our servants but if you win we will become your servants." All the men in the Israelite army were afraid of Goliath. None would fight him. When David saw how afraid the army was of Goliath he volunteered to fight Goliath. He told King Saul, "Your servant has killed both the lion and the bear; and this uncircumcised Philistine will be like one of them, since he has taunted the armies of the living God.... The Lord who delivered me from the paw of the lion and from the paw of the bear, He will deliver me from the hand of this Philistine" (1 Samuel 17:36, 37).

David prepared to fight the Philistine with only a slingshot and five smooth stones. When Goliath saw David, he roared and said, "Am I a dog, that you come to me with sticks?" David said to him, "You come to me with a sword, a spear, and a javelin, but I come to you in the name of the Lord of hosts, the God of the armies of Israel, whom you have taunted."

David used his sling to throw the stone at Goliath. The stone hit Goliath on his forehead and he fell dead. When the Philistines saw that their champion was dead, they ran as the Israelites chased them.

Discuss the story. How was David able to face Goliath and not be afraid? Why were the soldiers afraid of Goliath? What was the difference? What in David's life prepared him for this battle? How would you have felt fighting with Goliath? What things in your life are you afraid of? How can this lesson about David help us to overcome fear? As a family, list three things that you can learn from David to help you overcome fear? Why is it important for a leader not to be afraid?

David and Goliath Drama

The story of David and Goliath makes a wonderful drama. The four scenes could be: 1) David fights with lions and bears; 2) Father sends David to brothers (1 Samuel 17:17-25); 3) David volunteers to fight Goliath (1 Samuel 17:26-39); and 4) David kills Goliath (1 Samuel 17:41-54).

Rock Hunt

Some families might want to take a walk after they hear the story of David and Goliath. If you do, look for smooth stones like David would have used to kill Goliath. You might even want to make a sling and try throwing the rocks at a target. Discuss some of the same questions that are given at the end of the story as you walk.

Make a Giant

Use a large roll end of newsprint or a long sheet of butcher paper. Measure off nine feet, nine inches, which was Goliath's height. Lay the paper on the floor and work together as a family drawing Goliath on the paper. When you have completed drawing Goliath, have each person write something they are afraid of on Goliath. Hang Goliath on the wall and, as a family, attack him and tear him down. This will symbolize getting rid of your fears.

Family Prayer

Have a circle of family prayer, praying for each other. One way of doing this would be to have each family member pray for a fear of the person on his or her right.

> **Family Memory Project**
>
> Have the family memorize 1 Samuel 17:37 together.

Paul, the Leader Who Always Prayed

Family Fun Time Number

6

The Obstacle Course

Life is full of obstacles. Obstacles are problems that get in the way of living a good life. Taking care of or getting rid of obstacles makes us stronger.

Paul had many obstacles in his life. He was beaten, thrown in jail, shipwrecked, and was accused by his own friends of not being a true apostle. Paul prayed for guidance to overcome these obstacles and asked his fellow Christians to pray for him too. Read 2 Thessalonians 3:1, 2. Paul listened for God's guidance.

Here is a game that will help your family learn the importance of listening for God's guidance. Set up an obstacle course in your living or family room. Place chairs, pillows, toys, tables, etc., in such a way that a person would have a difficult time walking through the room blindfolded. Let each family member, one at a time, walk through the obstacle course blindfolded. Each person is to be timed. The object is to get through the course as quickly and clearly as possible. The person may ask others in the family for directions like, "Which way should I turn?" etc.

When each family member has had a turn, discuss the following: How did you feel when you were trying to get through the obstacle course? Did you want to ask for help? What happened when you asked for guidance? How is life like an obstacle course? How can prayer help? How does God's Word guide us?

Friends Prayer List

Paul always prayed for his friends. Read Ephesians 1:15-19 and Colossians 1:3-9. Ask each person to share the name of a friend that they pray for regularly. Give each person an index card and have them write the names of two more friends they would b willing to pray for each day. Discuss why it is important for a leader to pray for his or her friends. Have a circle of prayer with each person praying for the person on his or her list.

Praying Constantly

It is obvious from reading Paul's letters that he prayed constantly. Read 1 Thessalonians 5:17. What does it mean to pray without ceasing? Does that mean we have to pray every minute of the day and night? How can a person actually pray without ceasing? Why is it important for a leader to pray without ceasing?

Family Prayer Chain

To prepare for this activity, cut one inch wide strips lengthwise from a regular sized sheet of construction paper. If you do not have construction paper available, regular typing paper would be adequate. Each family member should be given one strip. On this strip of paper the family member is to write something he would like the rest of the family to pray for. Make chain links out of the strips of paper completing a family prayer chain. As you work on this project talk about the importance of a family praying together. Have a circle of prayer with each person praying for the request of another person's link on the chain. Hang the chain in a prominent spot and take a link off as prayers are answered. Watch the chain grow smaller as God answers prayers.

Scrapbook of Answered Prayers

Take some notebook paper and tie string or ribbon in the holes. Have someone in the family draw a pair of praying hands on the cover or some other symbol of prayer. Remember together prayers that God has answered for your family. Draw pictures or write the account of these prayers in your notebook. Add to the notebook as God continues to answer prayers. Take time to thank God for those answered prayers.

"Not Me, Lord"

Family Fun Time Number

Goal:
To help family members realize that God can use them even when they think they are incapable of doing the job. Choose from the activities those that best suit the needs of your family.

Part 2: Moses, Leader of the Great Escape

In this group of four family fun times you will learn about a leader with one of the most difficult assignments God has ever made. Moses was to lead the children of Israel out of Egypt to the promised land. In this series of family fun times, you will follow Moses—who was reluctant to accept leadership—to his death. Your family will see how God uses the reluctant leader to accomplish His purpose.

Excuses, Excuses

Explain to your family that God's people had been slaves in Egypt for many years. Now God wants Moses to lead them to the promised land. So He appeared to Moses in the form of a burning bush. But Moses specializes in excuses (don't we all). Hunt together as a family for the excuses Moses gives to God in Exodus chapters three and four. You might want to divide your family into two teams and have each team sort through a chapter. Next, play the following game:

Write each of the following requests on a separate piece of paper.

—I want you to be a missionary to Africa.
—I want you to talk to your friend about Jesus.
—I want you to ask forgiveness of the person whose feelings you hurt.
—I want you to give a devotional in front of the youth group.
—I want you to explain to your classmates why you don't do drugs.
—I want you to quit your job and go to seminary to prepare to be a pastor.

Fold the slips of paper and put them in a container. Have each family member draw a slip. Choose someone to start and have him read his request to the person on his left. That person is to respond with an excuse. This excuse must be completely ridiculous such as, "I can't because I ate elephant steak last night." Give a prize for the craziest excuse. Go around the family circle using this procedure until each person has read a request and given an excuse. Now discuss the following: Why did Moses make excuses? Why do we make excuses? In what ways are serious excuses and ridiculous excuses alike? What should our response be when God asks us to do something? Why?" How could Philippians 4:13 be applied to excuse making?

Exodus Snapshot Frieze

It's always a good idea to take pictures of family adventures; here is a fun way to do it with a "snapshot frieze." A frieze is a series of pictures that tell a complete story. Take butcher paper or newsprint roll end and cut an eight-foot section of paper. Mark off four two-foot sections. Now divide each section into four parts as shown below. Each family night during the month, your family is to draw four stick figure pictures about events that happened on that evening. For example, snapshots in your first section might have a picture of Moses saying, "But Lord," Moses with a staff in his hand, Moses with a leperous hand, and Moses with Aaron talking to the people. Assign family members to draw the "snapshots." By the end of the month you will have a delightful "picture show" of your adventure.

Predictions

It's fun to think of how God can use us. Have one person at a time sit in a chair with the rest of the family around him or her. Each family member is to predict what the person in the middle will be doing ten years from now. That should include job, hobbies, family, and especially what special things that person will be doing for God. Each person should have a turn in the circle.

Trust, Trust

Have each person finish the following sentences:
—Not me Lord, because (insert an excuse such as, " I'm too busy."
—I will Lord, because (an appropriate trusting response).

Discuss: which response felt the best? Write down one excuse you have used that you will change from "not me," to "I will." Share these with the rest of the family.

If you have young children (seven years or younger), read them the story of Moses in the bulrushes out of a Bible storybook (Exodus 2).

Have a play. You will need a box with a doll in it. Decide who will be the mother, who will be Moses' sister, and who will be Pharaoh's daughter. Here are some ideas for your play, but feel free to act out this story in any way you wish.

Have the mother pretend that she is making a basket. Perhaps the sister can help. Have mother place the doll in the basket and quietly sneak down to the "river" with Moses' sister and hide the baby. Now Pharaoh's daughter comes and finds the baby and Moses' sister runs up to offer a Hebrew woman to nurse the child for her. Moses' sister runs home excitedly to get her mother. They take the baby from the daughter of Pharaoh and take him home.

When you have completed the play, let your child draw a picture of the part he liked best. Talk about how God protected Moses so he could do a special job. Tell your children that God has a special job for them to do. Ask if they can think of something God might want them to do. You might need to suggest some things such as invite a friend to church or to be kind. Ask your children to decide on something God wants them to do today (perhaps some kind deed) and praise them for doing it.

Think Together

Discuss this statement: "What God expects, God enables."

The Secret Journey

Read or review Exodus 12. Catch some of the excitement of that moment by turning out the lights in your house. Tell your family to whisper. They are to go quietly to their rooms where they will find some coins on their beds. (Place an appropriate amount of money there before you start this activity.) They are to take this money and choose one more important item that is small enough to conceal. When everyone is ready, sneak out of the house, get silently into the car and drive somewhere for dessert. Let your children spend their coins for treats. As you eat dessert, let each person share what other item he brought and why. Ask what kind of things they think the Israelites had to leave behind. Talk about how exciting it must have been when the people realized that God had finally delivered them from slavery and they were headed for the promised land.

Here Comes Pharaoh

Tell your children that they will have ten minutes to record on the cassette recorder the sounds that might have been heard when God divided the Red Sea. Next, read Exodus 14 and have your children listen for clues of sounds they might record, (yells, noisy water, hoofs, horses etc.). Then let your children record and have them share their recording with the rest of the family.

Discuss how the Israelites felt when Pharaoh was chasing them. Do you think that they were afraid? Do you feel that they doubted God and wished they had never left Egypt? Have each person tell of a time when he or she was afraid and doubted God. What helps when we feel afraid? Does God ever let us down?

Pharaoh's Escape Tag

Do you want to start your family time out with excitement? Then try this game. Select someone to be Pharaoh. Pharaoh is "it" and chases the rest of the family trying to tag someone. A person is safe (cannot be tagged) however when he falls down on the ground, rolls over on his back and puts his feet in the air like a turtle. Pharaoh steps back three feet and counts to three. At this time the person may jump up and run away; once Pharaoh reaches "three" he may chase the person again. When someone is tagged, they then become "Pharaoh."

After playing for a while stop the game and tell family members that whoever is Pharaoh must now count to ten before chasing a person who has been safe on his back.

When you have finished the game, have someone review the ten plagues (Exodus chapters seven through fourteen). Discuss: How do you think Moses felt when he could not escape from Pharaoh? Did he become discouraged? How did you feel when someone decided to change the rules of the game and allow you to escape? Discuss how God is in charge—He makes the rules. All things happen when He wants them to. Ask family members to share times when they prayed to God for something to happen and became discouraged when things didn't work out the way they felt they should. And then God answered the prayer when He felt the time was best.

Goal:
To help family members see that when God chooses you to be a leader, He provides the power to accomplish His will. A leader should never give up! Choose from the activities those that best suit the needs of your family.

Pantomime the Ten Plagues

Write the Scripture reference for the ten plagues on ten separate slips of paper. Have family members draw the slips, read the reference, and then pantomime the plague. The rest of the family is to guess what plague that person is pantomiming.

Plagues Puzzle

The puzzle below contains key words that describe the ten plagues. Can you find all then?

Word List
FROGS
INSECTS
CATTLE
BOILS
HAIL
LOCUSTS
DARKNESS
DEATH
BLOOD
SERPENT

```
O  N  T  N  E  P  R  E  S
S  R  H  N  U  W  F  O  I
C  A  T  T  L  E  M  X  N
Q  D  A  R  K  N  E  S  S
F  L  E  U  D  B  L  D  E
R  B  D  F  T  O  E  V  C
O  L  I  A  H  I  O  X  T
G  Z  A  G  E  L  C  L  S
S  L  O  C  U  S  T  S  B
```

Discuss: Why were there so many plagues? Which was the most important plague and why? Does God still shows His power today in visible ways? How?

Snapshot Frieze

Have someone share highlights of chapters seven to fourteen. Decide which scenes you will draw and assign artists.

Pharaoh's Tag (Seven and Younger)

Plan a different version of "Pharaoh Tag." Determine a base where someone is safe. Appoint a person to be Pharaoh. When someone is touching base they cannot be tagged. Pharaoh chases the others in the family until he has tagged someone (or until you feel it is time to let someone else be "it").

When you have played the game, sit down and share with your children the story of God allowing Moses to lead the children of Israel out of slavery and their narrow escape.

"The Secret Journey" can also be adapted so your young children can enjoy it.

"Walking in Circles"

Family Fun Time Number

Campout #1—God's McDonald's

I suggest that you appoint a different family member to be in charge of each of the five "campouts." They should read the corresponding Scripture and have the room ready for the family to visit. You might want to limit the time spent at each campout to five minutes.

The first campout is God's McDonald's. The Israelites grumbled about the food so God gave them Mannaburgers and Quail-overs. Place vanilla wafers or other type cookies in various places throughout the kitchen to represent the manna. Instead of quail, place some pieces of beef jerky or lunch meat in appropriate places in the kitchen. Before your family has this feast briefly tell the story of "God's McDonald's" as found in Exodus 17.

Take a moment to thank God for the food He provides for your family.

The Israelites grumbled, but so do we sometimes. Show the grumble gauge below to your family. Have each person draw an arrow to where they feel their grumble level is.

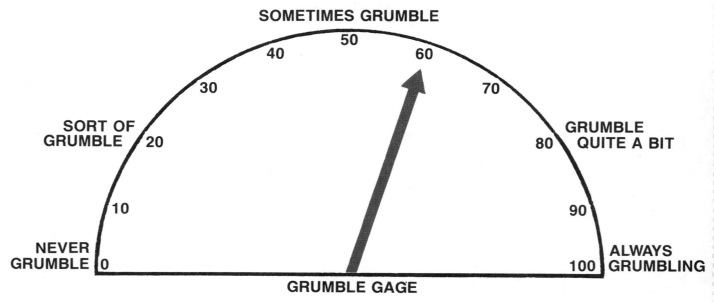

Discuss: Why do we grumble? Why does this displease God? What can we do about grumbling? Read and discuss Philippians 4:11. Have each person select a spot on the grumble gauge where he or she would like to be for the next week. Check the grumble gauge each day to see how the family members are doing.

Goal:
To help family members see the difficulties of being a leader and how a lack of patience can hurt affective leadership. Choose from the activities those that best suit the needs of your family.

Campout #2—Mt. Sinai and God's Commandments

This campout takes place at the foot of Mt. Sinai. Appoint a family member to be responsible for this location. When we did this in our home, Liesl, our then eleven-year-old daughter, placed a bean bag chair in her room to represent the mountain. To prepare this campout, the person in charge needs to read Exodus 19 and 20.

The person in charge may want to write the Ten Commandments on a scroll type piece of paper. The leader should read the Commandments to the family and discuss the following: Why did God write the Ten Commandments? Which Commandment is most important? Have each family member select the Commandment he or she needs most to observe.

Campout #3 — The Golden Calf

At this campout you will experience a real low point in your travels. While Moses was on the mountain talking to God, Aaron and the people doubted God and made a golden calf to worship.

To prepare for this campout the person in charge should read Exodus 32. Draw a large golden calf on a piece of newsprint or butcher paper. Tape it to the wall in the room you are using. The leader should role play Moses coming off the mountain and finding the people worshiping the idol. Discuss: Why were the people so quick to disobey God and make an idol? How do you think this made God feel? Was Moses right in being angry? When are you most apt to forget about God? What happens when you do? What can you do to prevent this from happening?

Campout #4 — The Tabernacle

Perhaps a picture of the tabernacle would go well here. A highlight of the wandering was the beautiful tabernacle that the people built to worship God. There are too many details about the tabernacle to talk about in just a few minutes so the leader should just pick out a couple of highlights (Exodus 35-40).

God told Moses to ask the people for gifts for the temple (Exodus 35:1-20). Verse 21 says that the people who really cared brought their gifts to God. People today who care still bring their best to God. Remind your family that gifts such as kindness and love are as important as material things. Whatever they give should always be their best. Ask family members to think of something they will give to God (perhaps their allowance, or a promise not to quarrel all week). If a family member chooses to give something of a non-material nature, the gift should be very specific.

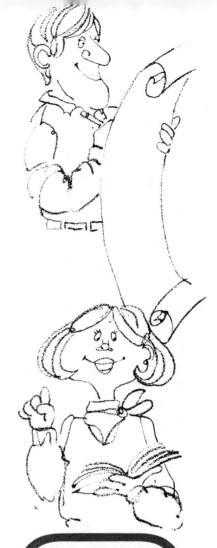

Campout #5 — Wilderness of Sin

The Israelites grumble again. (Sound familiar?) This time there is no water. God tells Moses how to get the water from the rock but Moses, as he brings forth the water, places himself on a level equal with God. Because of his failure to sanctify God, God tells Moses that he cannot take the people into the promised land.

To prepare for this campout, the leader should read Numbers 20. Have the rest of the family grumble about not having water. Act like you are very angry and arrogant and hit the rock twice. Then read Numbers 20:12.

Discuss: Why did Moses act like he did? How do you think he felt when God told him he could not go into the promised land? In what ways can our anger and pride cause us to disobey God? See if each family member can think of a time when they disobeyed God because of feelings of selfrighteousness. How can we learn to control our feelings? Have each person give a suggestion.

Children Seven or Younger

The campouts will work well with young children. Just simplify things. Most of the discussion questions will be hard for your young children to understand. But they will learn about God giving food from Heaven, Moses and the Ten Commandments, the people worshiping the golden calf, a beautiful building for God, and Moses sinning by failing to give God credit for His work.

Snapshot Frieze

If you are doing the snapshot freize activity, choose a scene from each of the four campouts to draw.

"The Promised Land"

Family Fun Time Number

Goal:
To help family members realize that God always keeps His promises. Even though Moses didn't get to live in the promised land, God used him mightily as a leader. Choose from the activities those that best suit the needs of your family.

Your Promise

Dad, say to your family, "I promise I will take you to the promised land tonight." Now this statement will probably make your family very curious and they will ask lots of questions such as, "What do you mean? Where? When?"

When you have finished any other activities you choose for this family time, tell your family to get in the car because you are now ready to take them to the promised land. Have a place in mind that you would like to take your family for a treat (perhaps an ice cream shop, a donut shop, or a special restaurant). Just start driving and let them guess where you are going. Change directions several times so they will be confused. After you have driven far enough to have them thoroughly confused and frustrated, stop at your "promised land." You will probably hear loud cheers.

As you have your treat, talk to your children about what just happened. Tell them that just like you kept your promise to take them to the "promised land" God always keeps His promises.

God promised the children of Israel that they would be given a beautiful land, and it happened. Because of disobedience, some of the people did not get to see the land, but God kept His promise to give it to the Israelites.

Ask your family to list some of the promises that God has made. Read or quote 2 Peter 1:4. The greatest promise God has given us is eternal life. Discuss our "promised land" (Heaven) and what you feel it will be like.

Some Activities to Do Before You Go

Some of you may feel like the activity I have just described is enough for family time. If so, fine. Others may want to do some of the following additional activities.

Snapshot Frieze

If you are doing the snapshot frieze activity, draw pictures of what you think the promised land was like, the spies, the crossing of the Jordan River, or the Battle of Jericho.

The Spy Ring

Moses sent twelve spies to checkout the promised land. Numbers 13-14:9 records their findings. Read this together and decide on the scenes for a family drama. Assign several family members to be spies. One person should be Caleb, someone else, Joshua (Hoshea), and a third person, Moses.

When you have completed your family drama, discuss: Why were most of the spies so negative about entering the promised land? In what ways were Joshua and Caleb different from the other spies? Why? Are we ever like the other spies—afraid to do things that look too scary or big? How can we overcome this?

Conquering the Land
(For Children Seven or Younger)

The Israelites had a lot of work to do once they reached the promised land. They had to fight many battles. The most exciting battle was the Battle of Jericho. The spies were sent to Jericho and were hidden by Rahab. God parted the waters so the people could cross the Jordan River. Then they marched around Jericho. This is a favorite story of children. Read the story from a Bible storybook. Set up the city of Jericho (a pillow) with walls around it (blocks, pillows, boxes or whatever you can find). You could even scale the model down and use dominoes. Have the children march around it seven times. On the seventh time, let the children knock the walls down. They will probably want to do this several times.

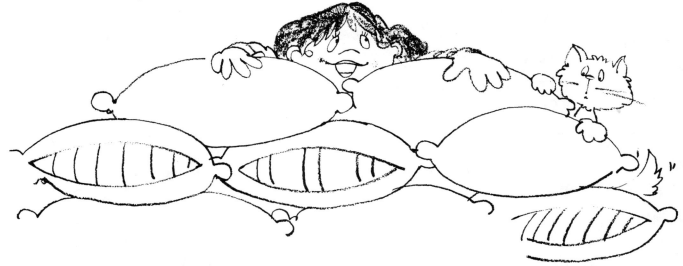

Part 3: Leadership Qualities

This group of family fun times focuses on some qualities that Christian leaders should possess. Have a good time together learning that you may choose to be different, live without worry, and love and honor others.

Leaders Choose to Be Different

Family Fun Time Number

Goal:
To help family members realize that leaders choose to be different and to help each person set goals for being different. Choose from the activities those that best suit the needs of your family.

It Takes Courage to Be Different

Explain briefly what this family time is going to be about and why it is important for Christian leaders to be different from those around them. Here is an interesting way to start your family time. Assign family members to be each of the following leaders: Caleb (Numbers 13:1-6, 16-33); Esther (Esther 4); and David (1 Samuel 17). Then these persons, in turn, should state who they are, what they have done, and read the famous statement of courage given in the corresponding Scripture verse. (Caleb, Numbers 13:30, Esther, Esther 4:16, David, 1 Samuel 17:32). The rest of the family should ridicule, argue, and coerce the actor into changing his or her mind while the actor shows courage to be different in the face of harassment.

After the three scenes, discuss the following: How did you feel when you were harassed? How do you think Caleb, Esther, and David felt? What gave them the courage to be different? (A few answers are 1) The desire to do God's will, 2) Courage, and 3) Faith in God.)

Share Your Pressures

Share some times when you have felt pressure to conform to a person or a group whom you knew was doing something wrong. What can help us in these circumstances?

Game—I'm Different (Based on Romans 12:2)

For this game you will need one index card for each person in your family. On one of the cards write, "I'm Different" and on the other cards "I'm the Same." Here's how the game is played. Shuffle the cards and deal one to each family member. Family members should conceal their cards. Next read one of the situations below. Family members are to react to the situation according to the card they have drawn. The persons holding the cards saying, "I'm the Same" will agree strongly with the statement while the person holding the card saying, "I'm Different" will not give in to the pressure but will be "different." Have fun arguing your positions. Talk about how it feels to be the only different one in a crowd.

Situation 1—You are with a group of kids at school buying candy from a vending machine. Sharon discovers there is something wrong with the machine and it is giving four candy bars each time the money is put in. "Hey you guys," she shouts, "free candy for everyone—the machine has gone wacky."

Situation 2—Some kids from the church youth group are discussing going to a movie that you have heard is very raunchy. Bob says, "Let's get a bunch together and go to the movie tonight, it couldn't be that bad."

Situation 3—It's "roast Joan" time since she isn't at the slumber party. "What a weirdo," says Susan, "Did you hear what she did yesterday?"

God's Standards

Read Romans 12:2. This verse speaks of the constant pressure from the world to conform to its standards. The pressure makes it difficult to "be different." The word, conformed, suggests a gradual process. Is being transformed also a gradual process? In what ways does being transformed help us to be different?

Reproduce the chart on the right on a regular size piece of paper.

In the first column, have your family think of some of the world's standards. For example, outer beauty is important, accumulation of money is important, success at all costs, etc. In the next column, opposite each standard of the world, put God's standard in that area. For example, God's standard for beauty is that inner beauty is more important than outer beauty.

Under "Degree of Difficulty" have each person rate themselves as to how much pressure he or she feels to conform to the world's standards on a scale of 1-10. For example, if a person felt great pressure to accumulate wealth they might put a nine or ten in that area. To conclude this activity, share ideas on what helps when a person feels pressures to conform to the world's standards.

World's Standards	God's Standards	Degree of Difficulty	What Helps

"I'll Be Different Goals"

Have each person set personal goals on how he or she will be different.

1. _____

_____

2. _____

_____

3. _____

_____

Leaders Don't Worry

Family Fun Time Number

12

Goal:
To help family members learn that Godly leaders trust God instead of worrying. Choose from the activities those that best suit the needs of your family.

What Is Worry?

Of course we all worry at times, this is natural. But many of us worry too much. To be used as a Godly leader we must learn to trust God more and worry less.

Go around the family circle and have each person give a definition of what "worry" means. Decide on a family definition.

God's Formula for Forgetting Worries

Gods Word gives us many principles to help us stop worrying. Ask family members to read the following Scriptures on what God has to say about worry. Psalms 94:12-19; Philippians 4:6, 7; Matthew 6:19-34; 1 Peter 5:6-11.

After each Scripture has been read, decide together on several important principles for the family to remember. Have someone write these principles down. Let these principles become your family's formula for forgetting worries.

Role Play Your Worries Away

Have each family member role play something that worries him, acting as if he did not know "God's Formula for Forgetting Worries."

Next, have that same person role play the same thing acting as if he had recently discovered "God's Formula for Forgetting Worries." *Memorize Psalms 94:19,* "Whenever I am anxious and worried, you comfort me and make me glad' *(Good News Bible).*

Here's an interesting way to help your family memorize this key verse. Have the family repeat the verse several times aloud together. Then write each word of the verse on a three-by-five inch index card. Shuffle the cards and lay them out on the floor. Have the family put them in order. You might want to see how fast you can put the verse in order.

Discuss: How does God comfort us when we are worried? How can memorizing this verse help us to stop worrying?

For Children Seven or Younger

Young children will understand the word "fear" much better than "worry." All children have fears. Start by telling about a fear you had when you were very young. Next, explain that even Jesus' disciples were sometimes afraid. Read or tell the story of Jesus calming the storm (Matthew 8:23-27).

Talk about how Jesus loves us and doesn't want us to be afraid. Explain that He is with us in a different way than He was with His disciples. Have your child share something that he is afraid of. Some children like to draw a picture of this. Talk about how remembering that Jesus is with us can help us not to be afraid.

Worrywart Pictures

Emphasize that everyone worries at some time. Have each person share the things he or she worries about the most, or the things they think other people worry about the most. Next, give each person a sheet of typing paper. Have everyone fold the paper in fourths. Each family member should draw a stick figure in a four part situation that illustrates one thing they sometimes worry about. Share and discuss these pictures. Discuss the question, "Why do we worry?"

Worried Acrostic

Have each person write "worry" in acrostic form on a piece of paper as shown. Everyone should think of a sentence that starts with each letter of the word "worry." These sentences should contain principles that help family members to stop worrying.

W Won't help anything
O Only makes things worse
R Really is silly
R Ruins your day
Y You can stop worrying

Worrywart Story

Have someone in the family start a story about a "worrywart." A worry-wart is someone who is always worried about something. At some point in the story, the first member stops and says the name of another family member who must continue the story. This procedure continues until every family member has added a part to the story. The person who concludes the story should end it using some of the principles learned in this family time.

Worry Less Goal

Have each person write down one thing that he or she is going to stop worrying about and one way to achieve this goal. Have a circle of family prayers with each person praying for the person on his or her left.

Leaders Love and Honor Others

Family Fun Time Number 13

The apostle Paul was a leader who delighted in the accomplishments of those he led. He was humble about his own accomplishments, always giving credit to God. In Colossians 1:3, 4 Paul says to his Christian friends, "We give thanks to God, the Father of our Lord Jesus Christ, praying always for you, since we heard of your faith in Christ Jesus and the love which you have for all the saints."

Christian leaders should give credit to God and give love and honor to others. During this family time you will practice with your family the Christian leadership quality of loving and honoring others.

Choose the activities that best suit the needs of your family.

Choose and Honor

Write each family member's name on a piece of paper. Fold these slips and put them in a container. Explain that you are going to pick out one name at a time and honor that person. The person whose name is drawn must leave the room while the rest of the family plans how they will honor him or her. The family reads the honor activities below and chooses several they feel the honoree will enjoy. Call the person back into the room and honor him or her. This procedure is repeated until all family members (including Mom and Dad) are honored.

Honor Activities From Which to Choose

• Notes of Love and Appreciation

Have each person write the honoree a note expressing love and things for which he appreciates him. "You are special because _____ _____." Go around the family circle with each person giving one special quality of the person being honored.

• Say "I Love You" in a Different Way

Each person expresses love in a different way such as a hug, a message, a promise to do something for the honoree, a compliment, etc.

• Compliments

While the honoree is out of the room, each person writes a compliment about that person on a separate sheet of paper. The honoree comes back in and one person reads all the compliments. The person being complimented tries to guess who wrote each compliment.

• Honoree Drama

Act out an interesting moment in the honoree's life. Choose a family member to act out an unusual characteristic of the honoree.

Goal:
To help family members understand that a Godly leader is more interested in loving and honoring others than taking credit for personal accomplishments. Choose the activities that best suit the needs of your family.

• Give Gifts

Each person gives the honoree a verbal gift for his life. For example, one family member might say, "I would like to give you the gift of happiness." Another might say, "I would like to give you the gift of a solid marriage," etc.

• Continued Story of Your Life

One family member starts out by telling something about the honoree's life. When he stops, the next person continues that story and so on until each family member has shared.

• Your Acrostic

Have each person write the honoree's name as an acrostic on a piece of paper. Each family member thinks of a quality of that person that begins with each letter in his or her name.

• Be Devoted to One Another

Conclude your time together by reading Romans 12:10. Discuss: What are some ways we can "be devoted to one another in brotherly love" this year? Have each person choose one of the suggestions as a goal for the year. In what ways can we honor one another during the year? Why is it important for leaders to honor others? How did you feel when you were being honored? how can we honor God during the year? Is honoring one another honoring God?

For Children Seven or Younger

Younger children will also enjoy hearing about the things that make them special. Family members might want to draw pictures of what makes that person special (such as his favorite activity or toy). Another way would be to cut pictures out of magazines or catalogues that illustrate the honoree's special interests or characteristics.

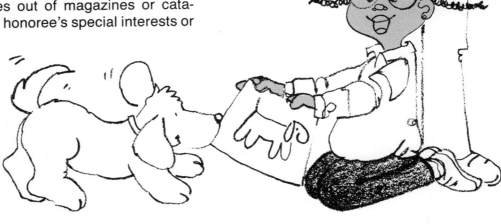

Part 4: Leaders Are Grateful

This group of four family fun times focuses on thankfulness, one of the most important of leadership qualities. Leaders are constantly thankful for all that God has done and is doing. The titles for the first three family fun times come from the poem by Cecil Alexander that inspired the titles for James Herriot's wonderful books:

All things bright and beautiful
All things great and small
All things wise and wonderful
The Lord God made them all.

Have a good time together as you learn to become more thankful.

God's Wonderful Creation

Psalm 104 is a song of praise to God for the many things He has created. Divide your family into two teams and see which team can make the longest list of things God created that are mentioned in this psalm. Underline each thing you would call bright and/or beautiful.

Give each team four minutes to make its list, then compare what you've found.

You Light Up My Life

God has made many bright and beautiful things that light up our lives, but each person is different and likes different bright and beautiful things.

To find out the kinds of things that "light up" your family, sit in a circle and take turns completing the following sentences:

Something bright that lights up my life is _____.
Something beautiful that lights up my life is _____.
When I see something bright and beautiful I feel _____.
The color that reminds me of bright and beautiful is _____.
Something unusual that lights up my life is _____.

Bright and Beautiful Tic-Tac-Toe

The tic-tac-toe game below gives you nine ideas for "bright and beautiful" things to enjoy this week. Tape the game to your refrigerator door and see how long it takes before everyone in the family can get "tic-tac-toe." Work to be the first in your family to complete three squares in a row.

Or, you may want to try to do all nine tasks together as you enjoy the bright and beautiful world God has made.

Count the colors of nature you can see from your living room window.

Get up early to watch the sun rise. Read Psalm 113:1-3 and sing praises to the Lord.

Lie on the ground and try to touch the sky. Can you reach it? Not even with your imagination?

Pick an autumn bouquet and bring it inside to brighten up the dinner table.

Gather a variety of colored leaves. Press them between pieces of clear contact paper and hang them in a window.

Start a sweet potato plant growing in a jar of water. Place it in a window that gets lots of sun.

Eat supper by candlelight one night. If possible, play an album of dinner music while you eat.

Go on a late afternoon walk and watch the sunset. Sing a favorite hymn as you consider the beauty of God's world.

Go to a store and take a count of the different fruits and vegetables available. Notice the variety in the foods God has created—so many colors, sizes, shapes.

Goal:
To help family members become more thankful for bright and beautiful things of God's creation. Choose from the activities those that best suit the needs of your family.

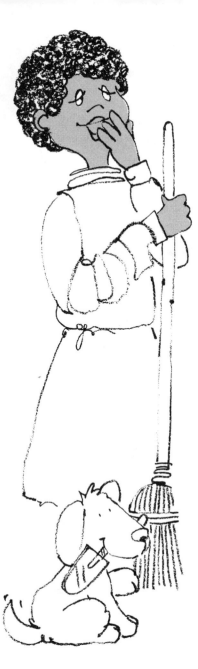

Work for a Bright and Beautiful Home

A home that is bright and beautiful brightens everyone's life. And, the responsibility for making it bright and beautiful belongs to the entire family.

Have a "brainstorming session" with everyone trying to think of as many ways as possible that your home could be more bright and beautiful. Include things that need to be done outside as well as inside.

Select two ideas as family projects for the next month. Talk about how you will start to carry them out. Don't leave the work up to one person; make it a family affair.

Or . . . Keep It a Secret

Have each person decide on one thing he or she will do during the next week to make the home more bright and beautiful. Keep your tasks a secret from everyone else in the family.

During family time next week, see how many bright and beautiful additions to your home the family has noticed. Have each person share what he did.

Do You See What I See?

Close your eyes and imagine that you're in a "bright and beautiful" place (perhaps a meadow, woods, mountain, farm, flower garden, etc.). With everyone still keeping their eyes closed, take turns saying, "I'm in (location) and I see (tell bright and beautiful things you see). Try to "see" the bright and beautiful things others in your family describe.

For Children Seven or Younger
Bright and Beautiful Place Mats

Cut place mat-size pieces of shelf paper for your young child or children. Using felt pens, fabric scraps, pictures cut from magazines, colorful trim, etc., help them make "bright and beautiful" place mats.

Cover the place mats with clear contact paper and use them—perhaps even on Thanksgiving Day—as reminders of the bright and beautiful things God has made.

Great and Small—Where Are You?

Start your family time with a Hidden Word Puzzle. Divide the family into two teams and give each team a copy of the following puzzle. Assign one team to find five "great" words and the other to find five "small" words in the puzzle. NOTE: The words may be spelled vertically, diagonally, horizontally, frontwards, or backwards. Which team can find their words first?

Hidden Word Puzzle

```
M  C  W  N  J  D  I  R  D
O  U  B  H  E  K  S  N  R
U  E  L  M  S  T  A  R  N
N  U  S  T  O  S  A  Q  T
T  O  L  N  D  O  F  D  G
A  P  A  D  L  A  N  T  E
I  N  B  E  E  K  Z  E  P
N  U  H  E  A  V  E  N  O
R  O  S  S  A  R  G  C  Z
```

After you have found your words, compare them with the list in the box on the next page. Discuss why you should be thankful for each of these things.

All Things Great and Small

Family Fun Time Number

15

Great and Small Walk

Go on a walk together and look for great and small things that God has made. When you spot something great (a large tree, a mountain, cloud, etc.), yell "great" and say what it is. When you see something small (pebble, flower, plant, animal, bird, etc.), yell "small" and share that discovery.

Have everyone find one small thing that he or she can take home. Work together and make a table centerpiece out of "small" things God has made (see sketch below). Be creative!

I'm Thinking of Something . . .

Play "I'm Thinking of Something Great or Small." Have each person think of one thing (either great or small) that God has made. Appoint one person to be "it." Take turns asking that person questions that can be answered yes or no until the great or small thing has been discovered or until twenty questions have been asked. Give everyone a chance to be "it."

Goal:
To help family members become more thankful for the variety of great and small things God has given us to enjoy. Choose the activities that best suit the needs of your family.

"Great Big"
For Children Seven or Younger

Instead of using the word "great" with your young children, use the word "big." Ask them to think of something big that God has made. Tell them to keep it a secret and see if you can guess what it is.

After a few guesses, let them tell you their secret. Repeat the procedure with small things.

The Biggest Smile

Have a contest to see who has the family's biggest smile. Measure each person's biggest grin (if you can stop laughing long enough!). Give the winner a "small" reward—such as a handful of M & M's.

A Word-Picture Verse

Help your young child say the words in the word-picture verse below. Repeat it several times until everyone knows at least the first sentence by heart.

God Is GREAT!

As a way to praise God for the many great and small things He has made, join together is this responsive reading of Psalm 145:3-7 from *The Living Bible*:

Parents: "Great is Jehovah! Greatly praise him!"

Children: "His greatness is beyond discovery!"

Parents: "Let each generation tell its children what glorious things he does."

Children: "I will meditate about your glory, splendor, majesty and miracles."

Parents: "Your awe-inspiring deeds shall be on every tongue."

Children: "I will proclaim your greatness."

All: Everyone will tell about how good you are, and sing about your righteousness."

End your family time by singing (in a "great" voice) one verse of "How Great Thou Art."

Word-Picture Verse

I bless the Lord: O Lord my God, how great you are! You are robed with honor and with majesty and light! (Psalm 104:1, 2, The Living Bible.)

Word List

Great—mountain, sun, moon, heaven, star

Small—ant, grass, seed, bee, sand

Wonderful Reading

Read Psalm 136 out loud together as a prayer of praise to God for all things wise and wonderful.

God's Wise Word

(Before the family time, type or write the following ten wise teachings form the book of Proverbs on small pieces of paper. Fold and place them on a tray so they will be ready to use when the family plays "King Solomon" during family time. References: Proverbs 10:19; 11:28; 12:18; 13:16; 16:24; 17:9; 18:24; 26:21.

The book of Proverbs includes many sayings of wise men to whom God gave great wisdom. King Solomon was one of these wise men.

Play "King Solomon" by selecting a chair that will be King Solomon's throne. Give each family member a turn to sit on King Solomon's throne and read a wise saying chosen from a tray of proverbs sitting near the "throne." After he reads a proverb, "King Solomon" asks: "Why is that a wise saying?"; "How can it help people like us?"

Take just three minutes to decide why each proverb is wise; then have the next "King Solomon" take the throne.

All Things . . .

Gather for a family prayer of thanks to God for all things. Remember together that,

"All things bright and beautiful,
All creatures great and small
All things wise and wonderful
The Lord God made them all."
—Cecil Frances Alexander

All Things Wise and Wonderful

Family Fun Time Number

16

Our Wonderful Bodies

Have each member of the family choose a part of his or her body and tell how wonderful it is. For example, it is fun to have each person start by saying, "I am (person's name) hand." Then go ahead to tell about his hand just as if the hand were doing the talking: "I pick up things. I clap. I write. I tie shoestrings. And I do all of these things without squeaking."

After everyone has had a turn telling something wonderful about a part of his body, find some lively music on the radio or put on a favorite record. Then everyone in the family can join in the fun of dancing around using all the wonderful joints and hinges God designed.

Goal:
To help family members become more thankful for God's wisdom. Choose from the activities those that best suit the needs of your family.

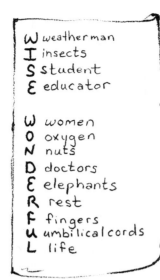

W weatherman
I insects
S student
E educator

W women
O oxygen
N nuts
D doctors
E elephants
R rest
F fingers
U umbilical cords
L life

Wise and Wonderful Acrostic

Have each family member letter "wise" and "wonderful" down the left side of a piece of paper in acrostic form. (See illustration.)

Explain that each person is to think of a word that begins with each letter. The words for w-i-s-e should be something wise. The words for w-o-n-d-e-r-f-u-l should be about something truly wonderful.

When the acrostics are completed, have each family member pick one word from his/her "wise" acrostic and tell why it is wise. For example, if the word is "work" the person must give at least one reason he thinks work is wise.

Next have each person choose a word from his/her "wonderful" acrostic and pantomime the word (act it out silently) while the rest of the family tries to guess what the word is. For example, if the word is "water" the person could pantomime a waterfall.

When each family member has had a chance to do both activities have each person read the other words on his or her acrostic.

Animals Are Wonderful
For Children Seven and Younger

Let young children name their favorite animals. Maybe some of them will be pets your family has enjoyed.

Talk about how animals are different—dogs wag their tails when they are happy, cats purr, etc.

Take turns acting like different animals while the rest of the family tries to guess what animal you are.

Draw pictures of animals that help people: cattle provide meat, cows give milk, sheep provide wool, chickens provide eggs, etc.

Read together the Bible verse: "O Lord, what a variety you have made! And in wisdom you have made them all! The earth is full of your riches" (Psalm 104:24, *The Living Bible.*) Thank God for all of the wonderful animals He made . . . and keeps making so we can enjoy them.

In Everything

It's a happy experience to give thanks to God for things bright and beautiful, great and small, wise and wonderful. But what about disappointing and difficult things? Are there any reasons to give thanks for them?

Discover the answer by decoding the following cryptogram. Compare your answer with the decoded verse found on the next page.

CODE: E = N; T = O; Q = E; 0 = T; Z = A

CTESIDQR IO ZLL JTY, MY BRQOHRQE, WHQE YTU

QECTUEOQR VZRITUS ORIZLS; KETWIEG OHZO OHO

OQSOIEG TF YTUR FZIOH PRTDUCQS QEDURZECQ.

Read this verse (James 1:2, 3), from as many different versions of the Bible as you can. Talk about what it means. Does it say that God can do something good for us even when things are going bad? What?

What are some difficult things you have gone through for which you can now be thankful? What is a difficult area of your life now for which you can be thankful?

Thank God for the Fleas

In 1944 Corrie Ten Boom and her sister Betsy were transferred to the notorious Ravensbruck concentration camp in Germany. They shuddered as they looked at Barracks 28 where they were to stay. The dormitories were filthy: somewhere plumbing had backed up, the bedding was soiled and rancid. There were no individual beds at all, just great square platforms stacked three high and from wall to wall.

Corrie and Betsy found the straw platform where they were to sleep. They lay back, fighting against the nausea that swept over them from the reeking straw.

"Fleas" Corrie cried. "Betsy, the place is swarming with them! How can we live in such a place?"

Corrie and Betsy's answer came from a Scripture verse they had read just that morning, "Give thanks in all circumstances."

"That's what we can do," said Betsy, "we can start right now to thank God for every single thing about this new barracks!"

Corrie and Betsy thanked God for four specific things. Can you guess what they were? (Answer: that they were together; that they had a Bible; that because they were packed so closely together, many more would hear God's Word; and of course, for the fleas—they kept the guards out!)

What about your "fleas?" Do you have problems that you haven't thanked God for? Read 1 Thessalonians 5:18. Have each family member name one of their "fleas" (problems) and give two reasons why they should thank God for it.

Discuss what Romans 8:28 has to do with being thankful at all times.

In Everything Give Thanks

Family Fun Time Number

Goal:
To help family members realize that Christian leaders are to give thanks always—even in difficult times. Choose from the activities those that best suit the needs of your family.

Decoded Verse:

"Consider it all joy, my brethren, when you encounter various trials, knowing that the testing of your faith produces endurance."

Pin the Tail on the Turkey
For Children Seven or Younger

Draw a large turkey, minus the tail feathers, on a piece of butcher paper or poster board and attach it to the wall. Cut out a large turkey tail feather for each family member. (See sketch below.) Have each person draw a picture of something he or she is thankful for on a turkey tail feather and share it with the rest of the family. Blindfold each family member, in turn, and have him pin or tape his tail feather on the turkey.

Mission Impossible?

Is it really possible to give thanks to God in everything? Read 1 Thessalonians 5:18 and discuss. Does this verse really mean what it says? How is this possible?

Part 5: Leaders Rejoice and Follow Christ

This series of family fun times is to help you focus on the miracle of God sending His Son into the world. Use one of these family times each week in December. Above all else, Christian leaders rejoice at the birth of Christ and follow Him in every way. Have a wonderful time celebrating the birth of Christ as a family!

Each family time in December there will be two Bible verses for your family to talk about and memorize. One will be an Old Testament prophecy and the other will be the fulfillment as recorded in the New Testament.

Each family time let one family member cut out a star you have outlined on construction paper. Print the Old Testament verse on one side and the New Testament verse on the other. (See illustration.)

The Prophets Rejoiced

Family Fun Time Number

Goal:
The goal of this family time is to help your family understand that hundreds of years before Christ was born, God's prophets knew that Jesus was coming ... and they rejoiced. Choose from the activities those that best suit the needs of your family.

Make an Advent Wreath

Advent is a special time for all Christians because it is the season when we prepare for the celebration of Christ's birth. Advent begins on the fourth Sunday before Christmas and ends on Christmas Eve. For many years Christians have used an Advent wreath made with candles as a center for family worship times held during the weeks before Christmas. Work together to make an Advent wreath your family can use each week before Christmas this year. (See illustration below.)

To make a wreath you will need a Styrofoam base, twelve inches in diameter, and at least one inch thick, five candles, four red, eight inches high, one white, ten inches high, artificial Christmas greens and any other ornaments desired. Use a table knife to cut five triangular holes in the Styrofoam base for the candles. (Make each hole a bit smaller than the base of the candle.) The white candle goes in the center, the red candles are evenly spaced around the outside edge.

Wrap the base of each candle with a bit of floral clay and push straight down into hole. (Don't wiggle it around or you'll make the hole too big and the candle will be loose.)

Use pins to cover the Styrofoam base with the plastic greenery and other fireproof decorations. (Note: you may use real evergreen branches, but they will dry out in a short time and become a fire hazard. Regardless of what you use, always be sure a parent is present when the wreath is lighted.)

When the wreath is made, do not pick it up by the candles, because they can become loose or crooked. (If a candle happens to loosen, use more floral clay or cut a new hole in the Styrofoam.)

Light the First Advent Candle

Let one of your family members light the first Advent wreath candle. As it burns, thank God for His Word that tells about the coming of Jesus.

Explain to your family that each week in December you will be talking about people who rejoiced about the birth of Jesus.

Prepare Your First Scripture Star

Make a Scripture star according to the instructions on page forty-nine, using these verses: Isaiah 9:6: *For unto us a Child is born; unto us a Son is given;* and the government shall be upon his shoulder. These will be his royal titles: "Wonderful," "Counselor," "The Mighty God," "The Everlasting Father," "The Prince of Peace." *(The Living Bible).*

Galatians 4:4, 5: *But when the time had fully come, God sent forth his Son,* born of a woman, born under the law, ... so that we might receive adoption as sons *(Revised Standard Version).*

Enjoy reading and learning the verses. (Note that certain words are in italics. Have your younger children learn only the words in italics.)

Use a thread to hand each star from a chandelier. Or save the stars to use as Christmas-tree ornaments.

Prophets Who Told of Jesus' Coming

Hundreds of years before Christ was born, God chose special messengers called prophets to tell the good news: God would send His Son, the Savior, into the world.

Following (in code) is a message about Jesus that the prophet Isaiah gave to the people of his time. Work together to decode Isaiah's words.

Message: — 8 3   ! ¢ 4 8   ! 9   O

_ _ _   _ _ _ _   _ _   _

½ % * $ ¢ *   9 2 8 3 @   ! @ 4 8

_ _ _ _ _ _   _ _ _ _ _   _ _ _ _

! 9 0   9 8 @   * 9 5 *   1 ? @

_ _ _   _ _ _   _ _ _ _   _ _ _

(Isaiah 9:6)

For Children Seven or Younger

Decoding the prophets' message may be too difficult for young children. Read to them from a Bible storybook. Show them a picture of a prophet and explain that God's prophets were happy because the baby Jesus was to be born.

Your young child might like to dress up in a robe to look like a prophet and say, "A baby, God's son, will be born." Include even very young children in cookie baking and other Christmas family projects. Plan simple tasks that will not frustrate them, but instead will help them feel as if they are celebrating too.

Standard Publishing has two coloring books, *The Joy of Christmas* and *Little Baby Jesus,* for young children. Also, *The Story of Baby Jesus* and *Thank You, God, for Christmas,* are two "Little Happy Day Books" written for very young children.

Sing a Christmas Carol

As a family, memorize, "Silent Night! Holy Night!" This is a favorite carol of young and old. Even a young child can learn this carol and enjoy the repetition of singing it often. Learn all three stanzas during the month of December. Young children can be taught all three verses of "Away in a Manger" by using the Happy Day Book of the same title from Standard Publishing. Each line of this old favorite by Martin Luther has been colorfully illustrated.

A	O	N	@
B	2	O	8
C	½	P	+
D	¢	Q	=
E	?	R	3
F	—	S	9
G	5	T	4
H	%	U	!
I	*	V	1
J	7	W	6
K	#	X	..
L	$	Y	/
M	()	Z	¼

John the Baptist Rejoiced

Family Fun Time Number

9

Goal:
The goal of this family time is to show how thoroughly God prepares people for important events, and how He used John the Baptist to help people understand why Jesus came to save us from our sins. Choose the activities that best suit the needs of your family.

Light the Second Advent Candle

Have another family member light the first and second candles of the Advent wreath.

As the candles burn, talk about how Old Testament prophets helped prepare people for the coming of Jesus before He was born. Explain that John the Baptist, a New Testament prophet, prepared people for the preaching and teaching of Jesus. He helped them know why Jesus had come to earth. Pray together thanking God for His love.

Meet John the Baptist

Read Mark 1:1-7 and John 1:28-36 to get acquainted with John the Baptist, where he lived, how he dressed, and some of the things he said. John rejoiced as he gave of himself for Jesus. How did he "give of himself?" What did he do and say?

Rejoice Through Giving

Your joy will be increased this Christmas if you concentrate on giving rather than receiving. Acts 20:35 says something important about giving. Unscramble the words. Decide what the verse means.

TI SI REMO DEBLESS OT VEIG HANT OT ERCEIEV

Discuss: What is the best gift you have ever received? What is the best gift you have ever given? How do you feel when you give a special gift? Why do you think the Bible says: "It is more blessed to give than to receive"?

A Birthday Gift for Jesus

Start a family tradition by making a "birthday box a for Jesus" to open on Christmas Day. Encourage each person in the family to make a card and place it in the box. On each card write, "Dear Jesus, I will give my love this Christmas by doing the following _____

_____
_____
_____
_____
_____
_____
_____
_____ .

In his or her note, each person describes the kind of Christmas project he or she will do in the name of Jesus for someone before Christmas. Here are a few suggestions:

Cheer up a friend who is lonely and unhappy.
Tell grandparents that you love them. Maybe write them a note or letter, or make a surprise phone call.
Make cookies to share with neighbors.
Surprise someone in the family by offering to help with a task.
Write a note or letter to a missionary.

Think up your own "giving to Jesus" ideas.

Place the cards in the box for Jesus and put it under the tree. On Christmas Day, open the box, read the cards, and have each person tell how his or her "gift for Jesus" worked out. If someone didn't get to put his gift idea into action encourage him/her to go ahead—even after Christmas.

A Scripture Star

Have one family member cut out a star that you have outlined on construction paper. See illustration on page forty-nine for an example. Print the following Old Testament prophecy on one side of the star. On the other side, letter the New Testament fulfillment. Enjoy reading and learning the verses together. (Note that the words in *script* are for your younger children to learn.)

Malachi 3:1 Behold , I am going to send My messenger, and he will clear the way before Me. *And the Lord, whom you seek, will suddenly come to His temple."*

John 1:29, 30: "The next day John saw Jesus coming toward him and said, 'Look! There is the Lamb of God who takes away the world's sin! He is the one I was talking about when I said, 'Soon a man far greater that I am is coming, who existed long before me!'"(*The Living Bible.*)

Sing a Christmas Carol

Let someone in the family choose a favorite carol for everyone in the family to sing. Practice all three stanzas of, "Silent Night! Holy Night!"

For Children Seven or Younger

Read the story of John the Baptist, "God's Messenger" from *The Bible Story Picture Book* (Regal Books) pages 108, 109. Talk together about the questions under the picture.

Mary and Joseph Rejoiced

Family Fun Time Number

Light the Third Advent Candle

Have someone in your family light the first, second, and third candles of your Advent wreath. As the candles burn, sing a Christmas carol and praise God together.

Have family members read aloud Luke 1:26-35, 46-55; and, Matthew 1:18-25 while everyone reads along or listens. Discuss: How do you think Mary felt when she first heard that she was to be the mother of Jesus? What joyful words can you find in Mary's song of praise (Luke 1:46-55)? How should we feel about Jesus' birth? Why?

Make Another Scripture Star

Cut a construction paper star. (See page forty-nine.) Letter the following Old Testament prophecy on one side of the star. On the other side print the New Testament fulfillment. Read the verses together and memorize them. (The words in *script* are for your younger children to learn.)

Isaiah 7:14, "The Lord himself will choose the sign—*a child shall be born to a virgin! And she shall call him Immanuel (meaning 'God is with us')"* (The Living Bible).

Matthew 1:21, "And she will bear a Son, and *you shall call His name Jesus, for it is He who will save His people from their sins.*"

Remember to use the Scripture stars for Christmas decorations—hang from a chandelier or use as Christmas-tree ornaments.

For Children Seven or Younger

Read to your child about "God's Promise," the story of the angel announcing to Mary that she would be the mother of Jesus from *The Bible Story Picture Book* (Regal Books) pages 88, 89. Talk together about the questions and statements made under the picture. Or you may choose to read "An Angel Visits Mary" from *A Child's First book of Bible Stories,* or "The Mother of Jesus," from *My Jesus Book. The Very Special Night* is a read-aloud Happy Day Book that tells the story of the first Christmas for very young readers. All of these books are from Standard Publishing.

Establish a Christmas Tradition

Encourage each member of your family to plan a specific way he or she can give or do a loving act for another member of the family. These gifts of love should be small services and kindnesses that will please other people—such things as, helping with kitchen cleanup, offering to do the dishes, reading a story to someone in the family, giving a sincere compliment, etc.

Be thoughtful and creative ... think up surprises. Perhaps each person in the family would like to use a "Remembering my Family with Love" plan sheet. (See illustration below.) Each person should have a sheet to complete by listing names of each member of the family along with his or her love gifts to them.

Light the Fourth Advent Candle

Light four candles of the Advent wreath, and leave only the tall candle unlit. As the candles burn, sing, "Silent Night! Holy Night!" Remember events of the Christmas story together . . . the angels announced the birth . . . the shepherds worshiped the baby Jesus . . . the Wise-men traveled far to bring gifts to the baby King.

Enjoy the Story of the First Christmas

Be creative in how you and your family share the Christmas story from Luke 2:1-20 and Matthew 2:1-11. Choose a way that involves everyone in the family. Here are suggestions:

Pantomime the story. Have older members of the family read the story while younger children act it out.

Record the story. Do you have a cassette recorder? Record the story of Christmas by having each member of the family read a portion. Even the youngest can be helped to say a few words. Then on family night, listen to your family read about the first Christmas.

Angels, Shepherds and Wise-Men Rejoiced

Family Fun Time Number

21

Goal:
The goal of this family time is to experience the joy of God's love, and praise God for His unspeakable gift—the Lord Jesus. Choose from the activities those that best suit the needs of your family.

Play Christmas Tic-Tac-Toe

Make a giant Tic-Tac-Toe game from poster board about two-by-two feet square. You can use the board plain, but children will enjoy decorating each square of the board with pictures of Christmas. Cut out some large O's and the other X's. Divide your family into two teams. If you have an extra person, let him or her read the questions. For each correct answer, a team member places one marker on the Tic-Tac-Toe board. The first team with three in a row wins.

You will need a list of about twenty simple questions based on the Christmas story and things your family has talked about during December family times. Here are twelve sample questions:

1. What Old Testament prophet said that Jesus would be called "Wonderful," "the Mighty God," "the Prince of Peace"?
2. What was the name of the town where Jesus was born?
3. What New Testament prophet helped people know why Jesus came to earth?
4. Who was the king of Judea when Jesus was born?
5. What town in Galilee was home for Joseph and Mary?
6. Who told the shepherds that Jesus was born?
7. True or False. King Herod was happy to hear Jesus was born.
8. What gifts did the Wise-men bring to Jesus?
9. True or False. Only three angels sang, "Glory to God in the highest."
10. How did they dress the newborn baby Jesus?
11. What was Jesus' mother's name?
12. What did the shepherds do after worshiping the baby Jesus?

Light the Last and Tallest Candle of the Advent Wreath

Save the lighting of the last and tallest candle of the Advent wreath for Christmas Eve. As all of the candles burn, read or repeat from memory Isaiah 9:6, John 3:16, and 2 Corinthians 9:15.

Form a circle by holding hands and sing a favorite carol. Pray together thanking God for His indescribable gift.

Make Christmas Stars

Have everyone in the family cut a star from construction paper. Letter 2 Corinthians 9:15 on both sides of the star: Thanks be to God for His indescribable gift!

Read the verse together as a prayer of praise. Work in teams of two, each person helping the other memorize the verse.

Use dark thread to hang stars from branches of you Christmas tree, or from a chandelier.

 ## For Children Seven or Younger

Read the story of the first Christmas, "Jesus Is Born," from *A Child's Firstbook of Bible Stories* (Standard), or "God's Best Gift," from *The Bible Story Picture Book* (Regal Books). Talk about statements and questions under the picture.

Two books from Standard Publishing for very young children, written in question and answer format, are *Jesus Is Born* and *My Baby Jesus Book.*

During the days near Christmas, take time to read other Christmas stories from Regal's *The Bible Story Picture Book,* or from Standard's *My Jesus Book.*

Encourage your child to thank God for sending Jesus. Learn the Bible words: He loved us, and sent His Son (1 John 4:10).

Part 6: Leaders Cooperate With One Another

Leaders work diligently with one another. Godly leaders must learn to cooperate with one another—not compete. The following Family Memory Maker Game will give you lots of practice at cooperating with one another rather than competing. The family must cooperate to move from "Start" to "Welcome Home." Have a great time!

How to Play the Game

The object of the game is to move from "START" to "WELCOME HOME" while trying to understand and cooperate with one another as much as possible. Only one marker is used—it is for the whole family. Each person will take a turn moving the marker.

1. To Start The Game -One family member draws a card, reads it aloud, and the family cooperates to follow the instructions.
2. When the activity on the card is completed, the card is placed on a discard pile, and the die is rolled (the same person who drew the card rolls the die).
3. This same person moves the marker the number of spaces shown on the die. Follow any instructions that are written on the block on which you land. After this two-step process, the next player gets a turn.

Remember—questions and activities are for the entire family to do together—not just the person whose turn it is.

4. Each player, in turn, follows instructions one through three. Continue the game with each family member taking a turn until you have reached "Welcome Home." We suggest that you end the game with a circle of prayer.

Make a Game of Making the Game

You will notice that the backs of pages 60, 62, and 64 are blank. This is so that you can remove these pages, color them, and cover them with clear plastic Con-Tac paper. (Color and cover the pages of activity cards before you cut them apart.) This way, you will have a colorful, semi-permanent Family Memory Maker game to use for many years. You can make a family fun time out of preparing the game, and your children will laugh in the years to come when they see their own juvenile coloring efforts. As you play the game, you may get more ideas for activity cards to further personalize the game for your family. Adding new activity cards through the years will also keep the game fresh.

Family Memory Maker Game

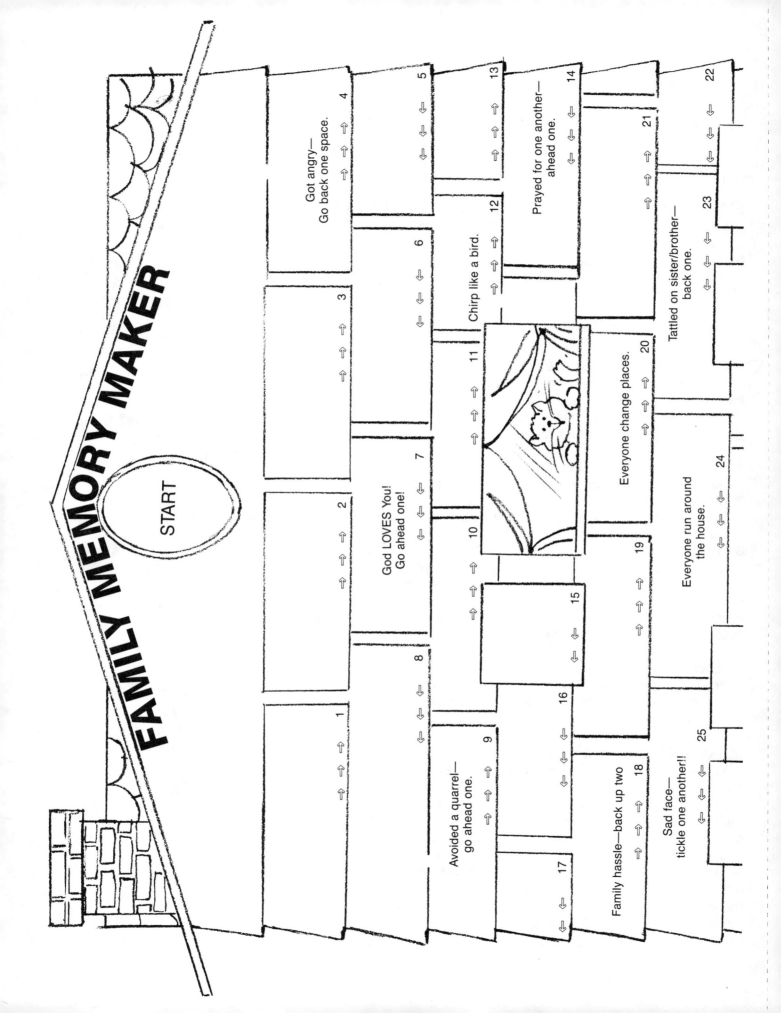

FAMILY MEMORY MAKER

START

1

2

3

4 — Got angry—
Go back one space.

5

6

7 — God LOVES You!
Go ahead one!

8

9 — Avoided a quarrel—
go ahead one.

10

11 — Chirp like a bird.

12

13

14 — Prayed for one another—
ahead one.

15

16

17

18 — Family hassle—back up two

19

20 — Everyone change places.

21

22

23 — Tattled on sister/brother—
back one.

24 — Everyone run around
the house.

25 — Sad face—
tickle one another!!

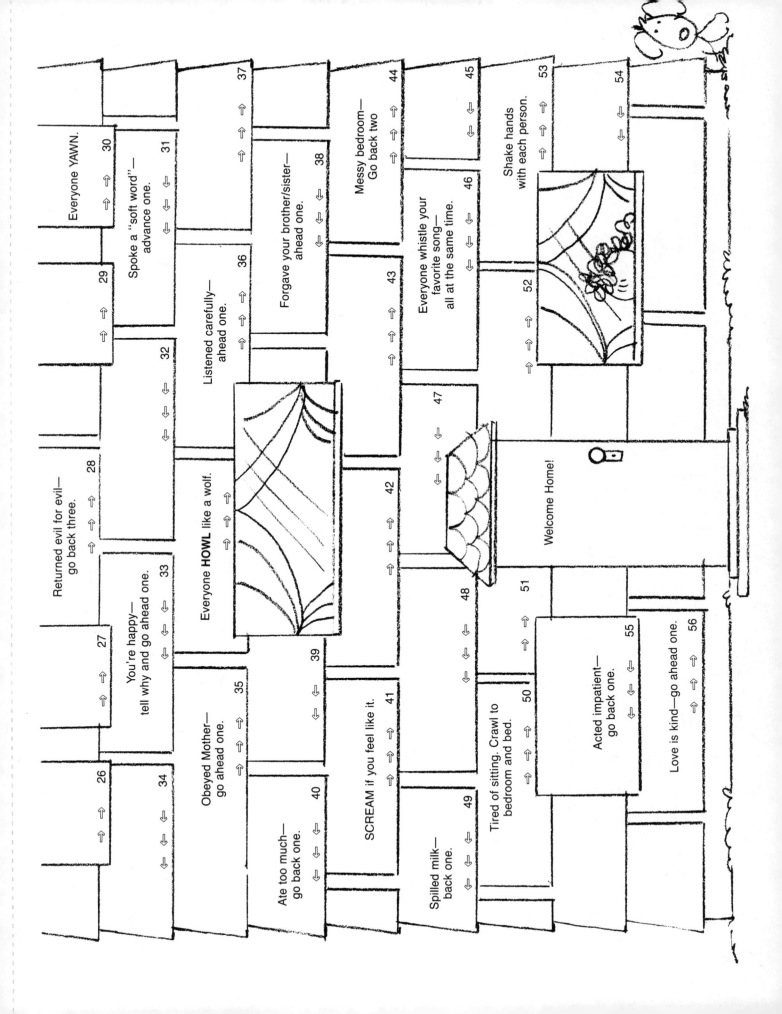

26

27 You're happy—tell why and go ahead one.

28 Returned evil for evil—go back three.

29 Spoke a "soft word"—advance one.

30 Everyone YAWN.

31

32

33

34

35 Obeyed Mother—go ahead one.

36 Listened carefully—ahead one.

37

38 Forgave your brother/sister—ahead one.

39

40 Ate too much—go back one.

41 SCREAM if you feel like it.

42

43

44 Messy bedroom—Go back two.

45

46

47

48

49 Spilled milk—back one.

50 Tired of sitting. Crawl to bedroom and bed.

51

52 Shake hands with each person.

53

54

55 Acted impatient—go back one.

56 Love is kind—go ahead one.

Everyone **HOWL** like a wolf.

Everyone whistle your favorite song—all at the same time.

Welcome Home!

Act out a characteristic of one family member—

If guessed, move ahead one space (30 seconds to guess).

The Bible says, help carry one another's burdens (Galatians 6:2). Tell about your biggest problem. Each family member, in turn must give you one idea to help you solve the problem.

Your family has just inherited $5,000 from a rich uncle. Decide together how it will be spent.

Agree on three words that best describe the ideal father.

If you could change one thing about yourself, what would it be? Each family member must agree or disagree that it needs to be changed.

What is your best family memory (experience)? If the entire family agrees in one minute, you may move ahead two spaces.

Agree on three words that best describe the ideal child.

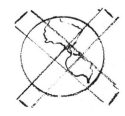

If the world was to end in one hour, what would be your final activity?

Think of someone with whom the entire family is well-acquainted and describe how you feel about him or her. If the family can identify the person in 1 minute, you may move ahead 3 spaces.

What is your greatest wish? If each family member gives you a good suggestion on how to get that wish, move ahead 3 spaces.

Find a feather. Together as a family, blow upward on the feather, and see how long you can keep it up in the air.

Join hands in a circle of prayer with each person praying for the person on his or her left.

Pantomime a Bible character. If guessed in 1 minute, move ahead 1.

Pantomime a Bible animal. If guessed in 30 seconds, move ahead 1.

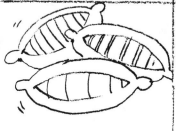

Each person go to his or her room and get a pillow. For the next 2 minutes have a family pillow fight.

The Bible says to "honor thy Father." Father must leave the room and the family must decide in 2 minutes how they will honor him tonight.

If you could have any person, either dead or alive, as a guest in your home, who would it be? If you can agree in 30 seconds, move ahead 1 space.

Choose a family member and have the rest of the family guess what his or her favorite color is.

Decide as a family which is the favorite room in the house. Stop for a moment and thank God for that room.

Say "I love you" to each family member in a different way (hug, kiss, smile, etc.).

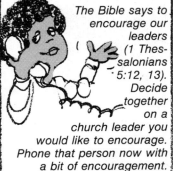

The Bible says to encourage our leaders (1 Thessalonians 5:12, 13). Decide together on a church leader you would like to encourage. Phone that person now with a bit of encouragement.

Have each family member complete this sentence: "I get a sad feeling when. ..."

Ephesians 4:32 says that we should be kind to one another. Each family member must tell one way that he or she will be kind to a family member during the next week.

All family members must laugh constantly during the next 60 seconds. If successful, you may move ahead one space.

Choose a family member and have the rest of the family guess what his or her favoirte hymn is.

Fire drill!! Everyone should go to their rooms and bring back the thing they would take with them in case of fire. Tell why. If done in 3 minutes, you may move ahead 3 spaces.

The Bible says "Be thankful in all circumstances." Agree on a family disappointment to thank God for.

Decide together what animal Dad should be. Each child may have a ride.

The Bible says that family members should be provided for (1 Timothy 5:8). Decide on a reasonable amount of money to provide for each child now. The wage earner(s) must agree.

Romans 12:13 says we are to "open our homes to strangers." Decide now on a family who are strangers to you, and invite them to your house for dinner or dessert—set a date.

God's Word says not to quarrel (Proverbs 17:14). When was the last family quarrel, and how can it be avoided in the future?

Exchange a piece of clothing with the person on the left and wear it for the rest of the game.

Each family member must find a hat and wear it for the rest of the game.

Raid the cookie jar— each person may have 2 cookies!!

Jesus said to follow His example. You are the leader. Family members must do as you do for the next 3 minutes.

This section is simply to help your family have a great time together. As you know, leaders can have fun also. In fact, a person who has the leadership qualities of a strong faith, individuality, courage, and the ability to forgive, is unquestionably someone with great joy. While most of the activities in this section are not tied to Biblical truths, they will enable you to build family togetherness; an act of love that will endow you and your family members with the qualities of a leader in God's church.

Simple Games for Family Fun

Some of our best times together as a family have been when we have played simple games. In this section, I'm going to share some of our favorites with you. Often we will play one of these games on a family night. Other times we will play a game after dinner or perhaps on a Friday evening.

It's good to have a list of games that the family enjoys. If you have such a list, you will probably find games in this chapter that you will want to add to it. If you do not have a list I suggest that you use this chapter to help you begin one.

These games take little or no preparation, involve plenty of action and are just plain fun. Read through this section and put a check mark by the games you feel your family will enjoy. The next time you are tempted to reach for the TV knob, try one of these games instead, and see if old-fashioned family fun isn't still the best family time of all.

1. Table Hockey. Ever hear of table hockey? I hadn't either, until a friend, Skip Centioli, explained the fun he had playing the game with his wife, two teenage sons and a five-year-old daughter.

It sounded like a good idea to me so we tried it on our next family night. The girls loved it. Here's how it's played: place two pieces of tape four inches apart on each end of your kitchen or dining room table as shown in the illustration. A Ping-Pong ball makes a good puck. Divide your family into two teams. You will need a minimum of four persons. If your family has an odd number, one of the younger children could help a teammate, or Mom or Dad could serve as scorekeeper and referee.

Assign goals and put opposing team members at each end of the table to defend their goal. Position the other players on either side of the table. Each team tries to blow the Ping-Pong ball through the opening between the tape strips on the opposing team's goal. If the Ping-Pong ball does not go through the goal but goes off the end of the table, the team trying to score the goal receives one point. If the ball goes off the side of the table, no points are scored, the ball is placed in the center of the table, and both sides blow on the ball again. Play this game for fifteen minutes or until one family member faints from lack of air.

2. Box Bowling.

This game has been so popular with our children that they have asked me to lead it at their birthday parties. Cutting in from the open top of a grocery carton, make three different sized holes in one side of the box. Cut one hole just a bit bigger than a tennis ball, the next hole two inches bigger than a tennis ball, and the last hole twice the size of a tennis ball, as shown. If you have very young children, you might want to make the holes even larger.

Place the box upside down on the floor. You might want to secure it by pinning it to a carpet, or taping it to a bare floor. Mark a starting line from five to ten feet away from the box, depending on the age of your children. Some families might want to stagger the starting line, with the younger children starting closer and the older children and parents starting farther back.

Each family member, in turn, tries to roll the ball through one of the holes. The smallest hole counts three points, the next two points, and the largest hole one point. The person with the most points wins.

3. Hide-and-Seek.

This is one of the oldest and most popular games with children. Dads, play this once a week with your small children and you will be sure to win the "Best Dad on the Block" award. Choose a base and have your child hide. Count to twenty out loud and yell, "Here I come, ready or not." If you find a child before he touches base, then he is "It" and must count while you hide. When our children were small, we just took turns hiding.

4. Ring Toss. Give each family member a two-foot section of aluminum foil from which to make a ring. First roll the foil into a straight piece, and then form a ring by twisting the two ends together.

Next, find three pop bottles and place them, one in front of the other, about a foot apart. These are the targets for the rings. If a family member tosses his ring around the bottle nearest the starting line, he scores one point. If he encircles the second, he gets three points and if he circles the last bottle he gets five points. The first person to score twenty points is the winner. Your starting line should be from five to ten feet away from the bottles; decide what distance is best for your family.

Another type of target is a chair turned upside-down. Assign a point total to each leg. Family members toss their rings over the legs.

5. Balloon Fun. It's amazing how many ways you can use the plain old balloon to have fun. If you always keep a package of balloons around, family fun will be at your fingertips. Here are some ways to use a balloon:

*Keep it floating. For very young children this will be difficult but fun. Keep batting the balloon in the air; don't let it hit the floor.

*Volleyball. Tape or in some way attach a string across a room in your house. Choose teams for balloon volleyball. Score like regular volleyball. Give the small children a chance to hit the ball. Remember that competition within the family should never take the place of being considerate of one another. Allowances always need to be made for younger children.

*Balloon Tag. Choose someone to be "It." He or she must chase other family members around, batting the balloon at them. When he is able to hit the balloon so that it touches another family member, then that person is "It."

*Balloon Football. We play this in our hallway and the children love it. The football field can be a hall or a room. Divide the family into two equal teams. The idea of the game is for one team to bat the balloon in the air over the other team's goal line without the balloon hitting the floor. The defense tries to hit the balloon downward so it will hit the floor. If the balloon hits the floor, the opposing teams takes over and tries to hit the ball over the opposite goal line.

To start the game, one team kicks off (hits the balloon toward the other team). The receiving team hits the balloon until it scores a touchdown or

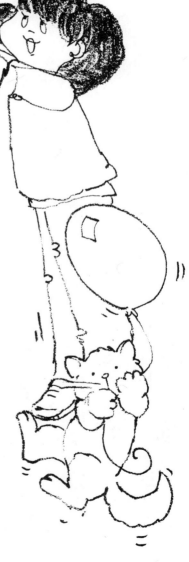

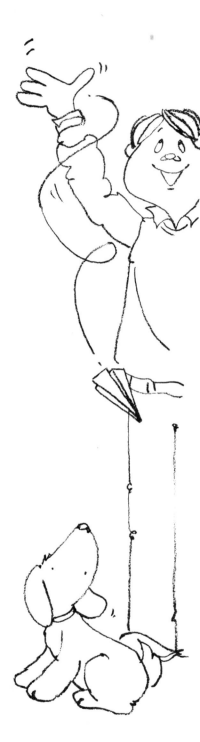

the ball hits the floor. Better set a time limit on this game. It can get rough.

*Balloon Soccer. Play balloon soccer like regular soccer. Simply set two goals and have teams try to kick the balloon over the opposing team's goal. Have plenty of spare balloons ready.

6. Holf.
What is Holf? Why, house golf, or course. Mothers, I'm sure you will be delighted to know your house can be a minature golf course.

Each room, except the bathrooms, will be a hole. If you have seven usable rooms then you will have a seven-hole holf course. Cut a two-foot section of string for each room you are going to use. Tie the ends of each section of string together to make a circle. Place one of these string circles on the floor in each room. Number your rooms.

A tennis ball will serve as your holf ball. Each person will need a holf club. Great flexibility can be used here as family members find something with which they can hit the ball. It can be a yardstick, ruler, plain old stick from a tree, umbrella, broom handle, etc.

Assign a par (the number of strokes it should take to get the ball in the "hole") of four for each hole. Each person should keep his or her own score on an index card. Starting with hole one, each person gets one stroke, in turn, until he gets his ball in the "hole." He then marks down how many strokes it took him. When each person has completed the "hole," the family moves on to the next "hole" using the same procedure until all have been played. Players total up their scores and the family member with the smallest score wins.

Be as creative as you wish with your holf course, and how you play the game. As your children get older and better at the game, you may want to place obstacles in the way of the holes, assign different pars, or make smaller circles. For very young children, you may want to make larger circles.

7. Paper Plane Aerobatics.
Remember the good old days when children used to make paper planes? This activity seems to have flown out the window and has been replaced with our modern, space-age toys, but old-fashioned activities, such as paper airplanes, when made as a family project, can be great fun. Here are some examples of what your family can do together on Paper Plane Aerobatics Day.

Each person makes a paper airplane. The little children might need help from the older, more experienced pilots. Each person should have time to test his plane to make sure it is ready for the contest. Here are some events to include in your contest.

*Blind Landing. Place a target such as a rock or stick if you are outside or a pillow or plate if you are inside. Each person, in turn, is blindfolded, and tries to see how close he can land his airplane to the target. Now try this with the blindfolds off.

*Airborne Record. Have each family member fly his or her airplane to see which one can go the farthest.

*Tight Squeeze. For this flight, have family members line up at the end of a hall to take turns at launching their planes. The idea is to fly the airplane down the hall without letting it touch either side. Place a pillow at the end of the hall for the landing strip. If the airplane goes down the hall without touching the sides, the pilot scores three points. If the airplane touches the landing strip, the pilot scores another two points. Give each person five flights.

*Airplane Catch. Divide your family into pairs and have the pairs line up ten to fifteen feet apart, facing one another. At a given signal, each person is to fly his plane toward the other person who is to try to catch the plane. For eye safety, use only blunt-nose models for this game.

8. Freeze tag. Appoint one family member to be "It." He chases the other family members until he is able to tag someone. That person must "freeze" in the exact position he was tagged. Other family members should try to "unfreeze" him by touching him. The game is over when all family members have been frozen or "It" gives up.

9. Did It Really Happen? Write the following statements on ten separate slips of paper.

    a. My most embarrassing moment
    b. The best thing I ever did
    c. The most interesting person I ever met
    d. The worst day I can remember
    e. The best day I can remember
    f. The funniest thing that ever happened to me
    g. The time I was most afraid
    h. My greatest accomplishment
    i. The funniest thing I have ever seen someone else do
    j. The dumbest thing I have ever done

Fold the slips of paper and put them in a bowl. Each family member draws out a slip until all slips have been drawn. Explain that family members must tell a story based on the slip they drew. This story may be true or false. While the story is being told, if a family member feels the story is false, he may "gong" (hit the lids of two pans together) that person. The person then stops his story and tells whether the story was true or false.

If the story was false, the person who "gonged" may ask the storyteller to do a consequence (like run around the house, stand on his head, etc.). If the storyteller says his story was true (and the rest of the family agree that it was), then the teller may ask the "gonger" to do a consequence.

This procedure continues until all the statements have been used.

10. Penny Toss. Are you ready to spend some money? If so, this game could be a winner for you. Place a large calendar (at least six inches by nine inches), at one end of your table. Give each person one penny. Explain that the object of the game is to toss the penny onto one of the days of the month. The higher the number, the greater reward. For example, if a person's penny lands on the twenty-first he will get twenty-one pennies. If the penny lands on a line there is no score. Each family member get ten throws.

Now, if this seems a little expensive to you, use some other good options. Instead of pennies, use peanuts or M & Ms. Or you can just keep score and name as the winner the person who scored the most points.

11. Paper Race. Give each family member two large sheets of paper. Determine a starting and finish line. Each family member is to race toward the finish line but may step only on the paper, moving ahead one step at a time. At no time may a contestant's foot touch the ground, or he is disqualified.

12. Pillow Fight. This is an ancient family tradition that always proves to be a painful delight. Sometimes I will announce that we are going to have a pillow fight, and other times the idea arises spontaneously in our family. Each person gets a fluffy pillow and tries to hit another family member with it. Warning: pillows can hurt if swung hard. The family must understand that this is just for fun and that pillows should not be swung hard at another's head. A family member who violates this rule must sit out the rest of the fight. Call time when you have had enough.

13. Table Ball Roll. You need four players (if there are more than four in your family you can team up) and two tennis balls. Position one team at the ends of the table and the other team on the sides. The team at the ends of the table tries to roll the ball the length of the table. The opposing team on the side tries to prevent this by rolling their ball across the table to strike the other ball. Score one point for the team that is able to roll the ball the length of the table. Score three points for each time a team knocks the opponent's ball off the table. Each team gets ten turns at trying to roll the ball the length of the table. Alternate positions.

14. Table Pool. Tape a Styrofoam cup at each corner of one end of your table. Tape another cup an equal distance between the two cups. The top of the cups should be even with the top of your table. You will need a Ping-Pong ball and a pencil. Each person, in turn, hits the Ping-Pong ball with his pencil, as if playing pool. The object is to get the Ping-Pong ball into one of the cups. The cup on the left scores one point, the cup on the middle three points, and the cup on the right five points. Each family member get ten shots.

15. Follow the Leader. The little ones will especially like this game. One person is appointed leader. The rest of the family must do exactly as the leader does. It is best to have a set amount of time for a person to be the leader. Each family member should get a turn at being the leader.

16. Plus and Minus. This game can be played inside or outside. You will need a two-foot square marked off in nine eight-inch sections, as shown below. You can draw this on the sidewalk or use a large piece of cloth, or butcher paper.

Number the sections 1-9. Find two flat jar caps or cut out similar-size cardboard discs; just about any small round disc will do. Write plus on one and minus on the other.

Mark a starting line three to five feet from the game board. Each person tosses the two discs. All numbers where the plus disc lands are added to the score and all numbers where the minus disc lands are subtracted from the score. If the disc does not land on the game board, the person deducts five from his score. Each person should get ten turns. The highest total wins.

17. Predictions. Each family member, including Mom and Dad, will get to be the center of attention in this game. Choose who will go first and have him or her sit in the middle of the room. Each family member, in turn, must make predictions about what that person will be doing in ten years. Predictions should include: job, family, accomplishments, etc.

18. Hang Tag. This is a very strenuous form of tag, and also a lot of fun. When a person is hanging by his hands from something (such as a tree), he cannot be tagged. Whenever his feet hit the ground he can be tagged. This is a good form of tag to play at a park where there are lots of monkey bars or trees with low-hanging branches.

19. Object Tag. An object such as a ball, stick, etc. is chosen for this game. The person who is "It" must touch the person who has the object and then that person is "It." The object can be passed by handing it to another person who cannot refuse to take it.

20. Favorites-In-Rows. Each person makes his or her own game board of sixteen squares from a regular-size sheet of paper. Here's an easy way to do it; have each family member fold his paper in half two times lengthwise. You will now have a long narrow strip of paper. Fold this strip in half from top to bottom tow times. Open the paper and you will have your game board of sixteen squares.

The game is played like bingo. Each family member, in turn, names a favorite thing such as a horse, candy, vacation, etc. When the word is given, each person writes that word in any one of the sixteen squares. After sixteen favorites have been given, the leader reads back the words from his or her own paper, going from left to right.

As the leader reads a word, each family member puts a large X in the appropriate square. The first person to get four squares in a row, diagonally, vertically, or horizontally, is the winner. Play this game as many times as you wish, perhaps changing categories each time, with the winner being the leader for the next game.

21. Call Catch. Have the family stand in a small circle. One person tosses the ball into the air and yells out the name of another family member. The person named must then catch the ball. If he misses, he becomes "It" and must toss up the ball. If you have smaller children, the person tossing the ball should call out their names occasionally and let them have an "easy catch."

22. Shoe Kick. Do you have a big backyard and some old shoes? If so, then you will be able to manage this game. Mark a starting line. Each person loosens up one of his shoes (or puts on a old one) and sees how far he can kick it. Measure distances and name the winner "shoe kicker of the year."

23. Predicaments. One person leaves the room and the rest of the family decides on a predicament. For example, "lost on a desert island." The person returns and tries to find out what kind of predicament he is in by asking family members, "What would you do?" The person must answer thinking of what he would do in that predicament. When "It" discovers his predicament, let another family member leave the room, and repeat the procedure.

24. Mimic the Masters. Have one person leave the room. Decide which of the remaining family members will be the Master. The Master leads the family in weird actions such as stomping his foot, sticking out his tongue, or scratching his stomach. The person who is "It" must discover who the Master is by watching closely when the actions are changed. The family should sit in a circle while "It" stands in the middle, watching closely to catch the Master. Let each family member have a turn being the Master and being "It."

Family Activities That Say "I Care"

How long has it been since you heard one of your children say to a brother or sister, "I love you"?

"What?" you say. "Brothers and sisters just don't do that." I'll agree that it seldom happens in most families. It's not that brothers and sisters don't love or appreciate one another, for I really believe in most cases they do. It's just that children do not naturally think about expressing their love and appreciation to each other. Wouldn't it be great if our children would express positive sentiments about each other as creatively as they express the things that bug them?

I believe we can teach family members to appreciate one another and to express it verbally. The most obvious way is through your example. How often do your children hear you express your love and appreciation for your spouse? Do you say as many positive things about your children as you do negative ones? Do you praise your children daily? Be expressing love to children in word as well as action, we teach them to express their love in the same way.

Another way we can teach them to express their appreciation to one another is through carefully structured family times that say "I care." Let's take a look at some ideas for family times in which we show our love for each other.

Family Times That Express Love

Our good friends, the John Drew family, have a family time each week that says "I care." Each Wednesday evening, in addition to to their regular family night activities, a family member is honored.

John, the father, begins by telling the meaning of the honoree's name. He then praises certain qualities in that person's life and sometimes shares a Scripture that represents that family member. Then each family member, in turn, says something he appreciates about the person being honored. The children are encouraged to look past outward characteristics such as pretty eyes, nice hair, etc. and focus on inner qualities such as kindness, diligence, etc.

"I believe this is the most important thing we have ever done in our family," John recently told me. "The children never tire of their 'special night.' I believe that this has been a great boost to their self-esteem."

"And by the way, Wayne," John continued, "each family member is honored including Carol (John's wife), and I feel it is just as important for parents to be honored as it is for children."

Family times that say "I care" help family members to verbalize their appreciation to one another, and this builds self-esteem. A good combination! I'd like to share with you some ideas for family times that say "I care."

1. Advertising Each Other. Write your family members' names on slips of paper. Put them in a container and have each person draw a name. Give each person a two by two-foot section of butcher paper or a piece of poster board. Tell family members that they are to make an advertisement about the person whose name they drew. Have a lot of different kinds of magazines available, marking pins, scissors, and glue.

Family members may make their advertisements in any way they wish—pictures of things the person likes to do, his qualities, etc. When the advertisements have been completed, each person should try to "sell" his or her product. For example, if I had drawn Bridget's name, I would have pasted pictures all about her—things she likes, her favorite foods, hobbies, qualities—on the poster paper. Then I would explain the poster, trying to "sell" the rest of the family on what a great person Bridget is.

2. Build a House. Write each family member's name on a slip of paper. Put the slips in a container and have each person draw one. Next give everyone a sheet of typing paper, pencils, and magic markers. Explain that family members are to draw a house for the one whose name they drew, as they feel that one would like it. It should be furnished and decorated in a way that reflects the tastes of the person for whom it is being drawn.

When we did this in our family, my oldest daughter, Heidi, got my name. She did a really good job of drawing a house that I would like—large family room, elaborately-decorated den with a large desk. But the moment of truth came when I saw my kitchen. There was an oversized refrigerator with guess-who standing there ready to open it! I could have done without that reminder of one of my vices!

When each person has completed his house, he should show it to the rest of the family, explaining why he drew the rooms a certain way, chose colors, decorated, etc. The person for whom the house was built should then comment on how well the house depicts his or her personality. Discuss how each person in the family is different. Take a few moments to thank God for making each family member unique.

3. Honor Scrapbook.
One evening a mother showed me a good idea for a family time that says "I care." It was an "Honor Dad Scrapbook." The mother explained, "Our children made this for their Dad on "honor your father" family night. The children cut out magazine pictures that reminded them of Dad. They pasted the pictures in the scrapbook. Under each picture there was a statement such as "Dad likes camping."

As I looked at this scrapbook of love, one picture caught my eye. It was a picture of a man and woman embracing. Under the picture were the words, "Daddy loves Mommy."

This would be an excellent project to honor your children. Work on this together with your spouse. You could cut out pictures, use old photographs, momentos, or write little stories of interesting things your children have done. Then, on a special honor night, go through the honor a scrapbook with your child. This could be repeated over the years.

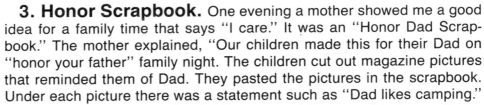

4. A Poem About You.
You don't have to be a real poet to write a poem about another family member. Just have family members exchange names and make a simple four-line poem such as:

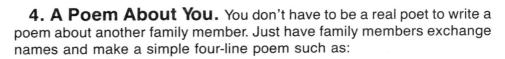

> Liesl can shoot a basketball
> Or run a very fast race.
> I'll admit she's very small
> But she sets a very fast pace.

5. An Acrostic About You.
Have each person write the person's name you want to honor in acrostic form on a piece of paper as shown in the sketch. Have each family member think of a quality of the honoree that begins with each letter in his name. Then share the acrostics with the one being honored.

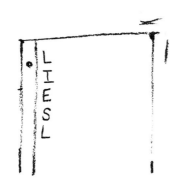

L —Lively
I —Interesting
E —Enthusiastic
S —Sweet
L —Likeable

6. Appreciation Night. Give each person a sheet of paper with a wheel on it, as shown. The wheel will be divided into as many sections as you have members in your family, including the center circle. Each person is to enter his or her own name in the inner circle. He then passes the wheel to the person on his left who writes in one section what he appreciates about the person whose name is in the center, and signs his name. He then passes it on to the next person who also writes what he appreciates about the one whose name is on the inner circle. This process continues until each person has written what he appreciates about each family member. The circles are returned to their owners. Each person, in turn, then reads aloud what the other members of the family appreciate about him.

Family members might want to keep these as a reminder that they really are loved and appreciated by other family members.

7. A Letter of Appreciation. We write letters of appreciation to others, why not to those who are closest to us—our family members? Take an evening to write letters of appreciation to one another. Of course, younger children will write very short letters, while older children should be able to write longer ones. The length is not as important as the fact that they put their thoughts on paper. If a child is having problems thinking of things he appreciates about another family remember, you might want to help him by asking questions such as, "What makes the person special?" "Does he ever do anything for you?" "What does he do that makes other people happy?"

8. Flower Honor Activity. Choose a family member to be honored, and have your family make a flower for that one. Draw a flower on construction paper and cut out the center and petals as shown. Write the person's name on the center piece and give it to him. Give a petal to the other family members. Each family member is to write on the petal what he appreciates about the honoree and give it to him. The one being honored then pastes the petals on the center piece and keeps it as a reminder of his family's love for him.

9. Pay Compliments. This is a game that gives family members an opportunity to show appreciation for one another while having fun. Send one person from the room. The rest of the family writes compliments about the absent person. The person who left the room is called back and one person reads all the compliments to that person, who is to try and guess who wrote each one. Each family member should have a turn being complimented.

10. Dress Me Up. Here is an activity that even the little ones will enjoy. Cut a life-sized piece of butcher paper or newspaper roll end for each member of your family. Have each person lie down (on his back) on the paper. Trace an outline of the person on the paper. When each family member has been traced, write your family member's names on slips of paper. Draw names. Each person is to take the outline of the person whose name he drew, and color in all the details. He should draw clothes he feels that person would like. Each person can add jewelry, facial features, hair color, and any other details. Crayons or magic markers work well for this project. Your children will be sure to "overdress" the person whose name they drew. You will have a great time laughing over these pictures.

11. Stick-Figure Appreciation. Do this activity around your table. Give each family member a piece of typing paper. Have everyone fold the paper in fourths. Draw names. Then have family members draw a stick-figure story of the person whose name they drew. Each person should have four scenes to his story, one for each square on the paper. Share these stories with one another.

12. Share a Burden—Bear a Burden. Read Galatians 6:2. Discuss: What is a burden? What does it mean to "bear one another's burdens"? Starting with yourself, share a burden with the person on your left. That person should say, "I will help you bear that burden." Then, depending on the burden, he should say what he is going to do, perhaps pray for you each day or help in some other way. Next the "burden bearer" shares his burden with the person on his left. Repeat until each person shares and bears a burden.

13. A Paper People Project. Give each family member a regular-size piece of typing paper. Write each person's name on a slip of paper and draw names. Everyone is to fold, tear, or manipulate his piece of paper in such a way that it will tell something about the person whose name he drew. For example, if I drew Liesl, I might roll the paper in a ball to represent the fact that she loves to play basketball.

When each person has completed the project, go around the family circle with each person explaining how the person whose name he drew is like his piece of paper.

14. Family Drama. Choose one person and explain that the rest of the family is going to do a drama about him or her. While that person waits, take the rest of the family into another room and plan your drama. Decide what event in that person's life you want to dramatize. It could be a great accomplishment or you might want to choose an embarrassing moment. When you have planned the mini-drama, perform it for the waiting family member. You might want to do a drama on each family member.

15. Great Moments in Your Life. Every family member has had some "great and memorable moments." Mom or Dad can share some of these moments at the dinner table occasionally. This type of activity can help build positive self-esteem and family unity.

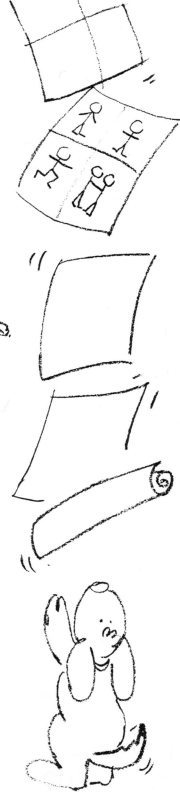

16. The King—The Queen. This activity is for children seven and under. Allow your child to be "king" or "queen" for the evening. Let him or her sit in the middle of the room while the family sings for him or her the following lines to the tune of "Row, Row, Row, Your Boat." fill in the blanks with the appropriate information.

> Heidi, Heidi Rickerson
>   (insert your child's name)
> You are wonderful.
> Your eyes are _____
> Your hair is _____
> We love you just like that!

17. Things I Appreciate. Have your family draw each other's names. During the next week each person is to look for and keep a list of the good qualities in the person whose name he drew. At the end of the week have family members share their lists. Who found the most positive qualities?

18. You're Like This Object. Each family member is to find an object that reminds him in some way of a quality in each other member of the family. For example, I might find a flower for my wife. I would choose this object for her because it would symbolize her efforts to make the house beautiful. For Bridget, I would find a picture of a person because of her love for people..

Communicating feelings of love and appreciation to family members is an ongoing process. Structured family time activities will help. Spontaneous sharing of love and appreciation is also important. Your example as a parent is vital. You can created a climate in your home in which the sharing of love and appreciation among family members happens regularly.

THE END